GREENBOOK ®

A Complete Guide
to Ty®
BEANIE BABIES™

Second Edition

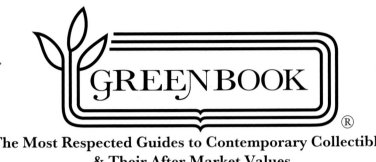

GREENBOOK ®

The Most Respected Guides to Contemporary Collectibles & Their After Market Values

2000 Sunset, PO Box 645
Pacific Grove, California 93950
408.656.9000
FAX 408.656.9004
www.greenbooks.com

ISBN 0-923628-51-7

Printed in Canada.

GREENBOOK TRUMARKET™ PRICES are compiled from trades and information provided by retailers, dealers and collectors. Manufacturers are not consulted or involved in any way in determining our TRUMARKET™ Secondary Market Prices.

Like Christopher Columbus in search of a New World, like Ponce de Leon in search of the Fountain of Youth, like the Pilgrims in search of religious freedom, Beanie Babies collectors have joined in their own adventure—searching for elusive treasures. Wooden ships have been replaced by mini-vans, spyglasses by cellular phones and gold doubloons with a gold card. But the passion for the "hunt" is no different, the excitement of the find still as exhilarating as it was to those long-ago adventurers!

The Beanie Babies Adventure has been fun for us this past year as well. We really enjoy receiving all your letters. And love hearing about your favorite Beanies and why they are your favorites as well as learning which Beanie you want the "mostest" but don't yet have. The pictures you've drawn and stories you've sent are terrific. We've selected a few pieces of mail from the thousands we've received to be included in the Guide.

Along with your nice letters, we've gotten a lot of questions from you over the past months since the First Edition of "My First GREENBOOK: The First, Original, Complete Guide to Ty™ Beanie Babies™" was published in 1997. We'll answer some of them here, and more of them in a new feature of the book—BEANIE-FAQs—(Frequently Asked Questions).

Because many of you have asked, we'd like to explain that GREENBOOK does not sell Beanie Babies. We publish guides to contemporary collectibles. That's all we do, and we do it better than anyone else. Since we don't buy and sell Beanie Babies (or any other collectible) we are able to give you, our readers, an unbiased opinion and analysis of the current market trends and prices. When we report secondary prices we determine those prices based on current secondary market activity. In addition, we do not gaze into a crystal ball to predict, as some do, what may happen to the price of a particular Beanie in the future. We feel it is irresponsible to publish such "information." We believe that your decision to purchase an item should be based on the fact that you a) like it and want to add it to your collection, and, b) that you know what the current market price for an item is, and are willing to meet that price. Don't be led into making a purchase by a prediction of a future higher price for an item.

In this Guide, all current Beanie Babies have a GREENBOOK TruMarket Value equal to their Suggested Retail Price of $5. While we are very much aware that many stores charge anywhere from $5 to $8 for current Beanie Babies, and in many cases more for the hard-to-find Beanies, we do not print secondary market prices for current items. The availability of any current Beanie changes on a day-to-day basis. What may be considered hard-to-find today may be available in abundance tomorrow. Patience is often rewarded.

NOTE FROM THE PUBLISHER (cont.)

GREENBOOK terms earlier versions of current Beanie Babies as "Out Of Production" because the design is not retired — it's just undergone change. And, in some cases, production of a current Beanie has returned to an earlier version.

In more and more instances, Beanie Babies are being used as promotional items for sporting events, fundraisers, etc. Organizations are buying cases of a particular Beanie and adding their own little touches. GREENBOOK limits listings in the Guide to promotions sanctioned by Ty.

NEW IN THIS EDITION

In this Edition, we've added information indicating which Swing Tags (#1 - #5) are/were available on each Beanie.

Remember, all tags (#1 - #5) are/were not necessarily available on every Beanie. Before purchasing an expensive Beanie Baby, make sure that a correct Swing Tag is attached.

If you own the Premiere Edition of this Guide, you'll also notice we've added the GBTru History Line. This line documents the secondary market history of each Beanie (currently one year).

Thanks for buying the guide—

Louise Langenfeld

Editor & Publisher

GREENBOOK would like to thank
all the retailers and collectors who contributed to
this Guide with a special thanks to
Frank Gimber.

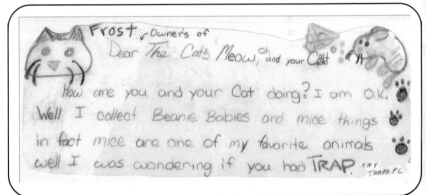

Frost, Owner's of
Dear The Cats Meow, oh, and your Cat

How are you and your Cat doing? I am O.K.
Well I collect Beanie Babies and mice things
in fact mice are one of my favorite animals
well I was wondering if you had TRAP. KAY TAMPA FL

With thanks to...
The Cat's Meow

Rich & Lana Gernady, owners of The Cat's Meow & Jack Frost, resident cat.

Once upon a time, there was a favorite saying which parents — in fact, adults in general — used with great frequency. That well-worn saying was, "Children should be seen, and not heard." Ask Rich and Lana Gernady, owners of The Cat's Meow gift shop in Glenview, Illinois about that old saying, and they will readily admit that they are glad they DID listen to the children who visited their shop.

It is certain that Rich and Lana do listen, and will continue to listen to their young customers' requests and questions. These youngsters were the ones who brought TY Beanie Babies to Rich and Lana's attention. When the children first started asking for Beanie Babies, the Gernadys had no idea what they were talking about. What was a "Beanie Baby?"

Curiosity aroused, Rich went shopping for information. Lucky the ladybug was the first Beanie Baby he purchased. He gave it to Lana, commenting that he hoped it would bring them luck!

Since the arrival of that first Beanie Baby at The Cat's Meow, Rich and Lana have welcomed visitors – adults and children alike – from all parts of the country, who come to see their complete collection of every Beanie Baby ever made. Other than in photographs, many of their visitors have never seen some of the styles and variations in the Beanie Babies line. Many a "wish list" is conveyed to parents and grandparents when excited children see a Humphrey the camel or a Peace the bear for the first time.

Lucky the ladybug seems to have done her job in bringing luck to the Gernadys, who began carrying Beanie Babies soon after the arrival of Lucky. "Beanies are magical," says Lana. "These adorable bean-filled animals are popular with everyone from babies to grandmas and grandpas. Kids use their allowance money to buy them. Parents and grandparents buy them to use as gifts and rewards. Teachers use them in many educational ways. No matter what age the "kids" are, people just seem to love them."

It took a bit of time and effort on the part of the Gernadys to convince their customers that these charming animals were "collectible." Their first efforts in this direction were to compile a list of all the Beanie Babies — whether retired, out of production or current. Soon children were making their first ventures into becoming collectors. With the checklist in hand, they were able to keep track of the Beanie Babies they had, and let family and friends know the ones they wanted for their collections. The children quickly discovered the fun of the search and the thrill of the find!

From this idea, the Gernadys took Beanie Babies to a craft fair, still working to build the idea of collectability. Their next step was to take them to a collectibles show, where dealers and collectibles experts laughed at what the Gernadys were predicting was going to happen with Beanie Babies. It wasn't long before these experts were no longer laughing, as Beanie Babies quickly became the drawing card for collectibles shows — and soon, collectibles shows exclusively for Beanie Babies popped up across the country.

Rich and Lana's store has been called the "first true Beanie Babies Museum in the country." In a July, 1995 People magazine interview, Rich was quoted as saying of Beanie Babies, "I love them. There must be one which appeals to everyone, whether it is because of the style, color, or birthdate. It is impossible not to like one, and then you are hooked!" His excitement for Beanie Babies is contagious, and many have caught the bug. Customers who began collecting Beanies at The Cat's Meow occasionally remind him of how he tried to get them started collecting Beanies earlier and reflect on how sorry they are that they didn't listen.

Rich and Lana invite you to stop in for a visit if you're ever in the North Chicago area. Many of the Beanie Babies photographed for this book were photographed from their collection at The Cat's Meow.

And if you do drop by, make sure you meet Jack Frost, The Cat's Meow's resident cat. Legend has it that Jack Frost was the model for the recently retired Flip.

The Cat's Meow, 1814 Glenview Road, Glenview, IL 60025 Phone: (847)657-6369 Fax: (847)657-9368

BEANIE-FAQs

Who invented Beanie Babies?

Beanie Babies are the invention of Mr. Ty Warner, owner of TY, Inc., an Oakbrook, Illinois based toy company which specializes in beautiful, yet affordable stuffed animals. Beanie Babies are rumored to be direct descendants of another charming TY product, Pillow Pals, many of which bear a striking resemblance to Beanie Babies, although they don't share the same names.

Why did Beanie Babies get invented?

Mr. Warner invented Beanie Babies in 1993. His idea was to make a toy which would be cute and affordable, so children could save their allowance and purchase them. He described Beanie Babies as "pocket-sized, non-violent, non-computerized, gender neutral, affordable stuffed animals which introduce a huge sampling of the world's animals to children, and encourage compassion and education."

What were the first Beanie Babies ever made?

There were nine Beanie Babies in the original group. They were Chocolate, Cubby, Flash, Legs, Splash, Spot, Squealer, Patti and Pinchers.

Where can I buy Beanie Babies?

Beanie Babies can be found at all kinds of interesting places. Most people start looking for them at their local card and gift shops. But you can find them in other places, as well. They've been reported in airport and resort gift shops, children's clothing stores, florist shops, hospital gift shops and drugstores. You might even check out the gift shop at your local museum, aquarium or zoo!

Once you find stores which carry Beanie Babies, you will find that they want you to know when their Beanie Babies have arrived. Many stores post bright, colorful signs in their windows announcing the arrival of Beanie Babies. As soon as the shipment is sold out, the signs disappear until the next shipment arrives. You'll also find that many stores have Beanie Babies hotlines set up. A voice mail system answers the special phone line, and tells you whether or not they have received a Beanie Babies shipment that day, and sometimes they even tell you which Beanie Babies have arrived!

If you or a family member is traveling overseas, you might want to look for Beanie Babies in other countries, as well. Beanie Babies are also sold in Canada, the United Kingdom and Germany!

Why are Beanie Babies so hard to find?

Beanie Babies are incredibly popular, and everyone seems to want them. When a shipment of Beanie Babies arrives at a store, it isn't long before the word spreads.

While many stores just put their Beanie Babies out and let people purchase as many of each as they want, some limit the number of Beanies which can be purchased by an individual. Many stores keep a waiting list and are willing to write down your name and let you know when the Beanie Babies you are looking for arrive.

What is inside my Beanie Babies?

Beanie Babies are filled with polyester fiberfill and PCV (polyvinyl chloride) pellets, which are called "beans," even though they are really plastic!

Why are my Beanie Babies so squishy?

Beanie Babies are purposely underfilled with "beans" so that you can shape them into different poses. Some Beanie Babies, such as the final ship-ments of Legs the frog, seem to have more "beans" in them than previ-ous versions.

What does it mean when they "retire" a Beanie Baby?

Retirement of a Beanie Babies design is an honor for that Beanie Baby! It means that he or she will never be made again.

How do I find out when my Beanie Babies are retired?

Part of the fun of collecting Beanie Babies is guessing when a retirement is going to happen, and when new designs of Beanie Babies are going to be announced. The best sources for information are the stores where you purchase your Beanie Babies, and TY's website on the Internet.

A good place to check out for "hints" that big news is about to happen is the Internet Diary, hosted by a different Beanie Baby each month.

BEANIE BABIES FAQ

How do I get to the TY website, and what will I find there?

You can find the TY site at www.ty.com and on it, you will find all kinds of interesting things to do. Each month, a special Beanie Baby is chosen to keep a diary. You can read the entries, for example, in Spunky's Internet Diary for January, 1998, or you can go back and read diary entries for almost an entire year. You can send e-mail (electronic mail) to the Beanie Baby in the spotlight as well.

You can also receive your own USER ID from the "Beanie Connection," where you can post notes on the "Guestbook" to be read by other Beanie Babies collectors around the world. In fact, there are so many people who use the Guestbook, it has to be backed up and all messages deleted once every hour in order to make room for all the messages! (That's kind of like filling up an entire notebook with your school notes once an hour, and having to start another book - 24 books a day!)

Where can I find older, retired Beanie Babies?

Because Beanie Babies are so popular, places to purchase older Beanie Babies are popping up in many areas. Watch your local newspaper for announcements of Beanie Babies swap 'n sells at local malls and auditoriums. These are shows where people who have Beanie Babies to sell rent tables and display their Beanie Babies for you to come and look, and hopefully buy some of their treasures. The classified advertising section of your newspaper, usually in the "collectibles" section, probably also has a lot of ads in it, listing people who have Beanie Babies for sale. And again, the Internet is an electronic marketplace with many, many people selling Beanie Babies.

What about the Beanie Babies I own which have the wrong tags on them?

Probably the most "famous" tag switching error was the first shipment of Waves and Echo. Both of these Beanie Babies arrived wearing the other one's tags. There are collectors who enjoy having these types of oddities in their collections, and are sometimes willing to pay a little bit more to get them. But many collectors like to have "perfect" Beanie Babies — ones which are wearing both the correct swing tag and the correct body tag. It's really a matter of what you like to have in your collection.

One of the new additions to this book is swing tag information for each Beanie Babies design in the collection. This is to help you understand which tags belong on which Beanie Babies. You have probably noticed that the swing tag can easily fall off or be removed from your Beanie Babies. This means that if someone wants to switch the tags to create an "unusual" Beanie Baby, it would be very easy to do.

HOW TO READ A LISTING

The GREENBOOK ARTCHARTS & LISTINGS developed for the BEANIE BABIES Collection feature color photographs, factual information and GREENBOOK TRUMARKET PRICES. The ARTCHARTS & LISTINGS are in alphabetical order by Beanie Baby Name.

The specific factual information includes Name, Item Number, Date Issued, Ty Swing Tags Available, Status, Description, Birthday and Poem.

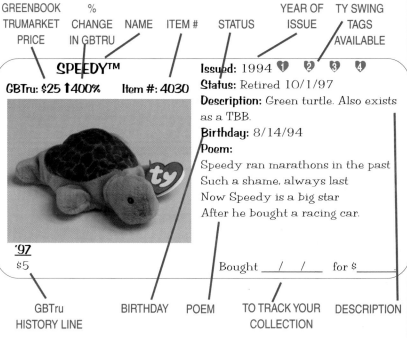

GREENBOOK TRUMARKET PRICE | % CHANGE IN GBTRU | NAME | ITEM # | STATUS | YEAR OF ISSUE | TY SWING TAGS AVAILABLE

SPEEDY™

GBTru: $25 ↑400%   Item #: 4030

Issued: 1994 ❤ ❤ ❤ ❤
Status: Retired 10/1/97
Description: Green turtle. Also exists as a TBB.
Birthday: 8/14/94
Poem:
Speedy ran marathons in the past
Such a shame, always last
Now Speedy is a big star
After he bought a racing car.

'97
$5

Bought ___ / ___ / ___ for $_____.

GBTru HISTORY LINE | BIRTHDAY | POEM | TO TRACK YOUR COLLECTION | DESCRIPTION

GREENBOOK TRUMARKET PRICES (GBTru)

All current Beanies are listed with a GBTru equal to their Suggested Retail Price of $5. (Please see **Note From Publisher** on page 3.)

Secondary Market Prices are reported to us by retailers and collectors. The data is compiled, checked for accuracy, and a **GREENBOOK TRUMARKET PRICE** established as a benchmark as a result of this research. There are many factors which determine the price a collector will pay for a piece and most acquisitions are a matter of personal judgment. The price will fluctuate with the time of year, section of the country and type of sale. **GREENBOOK** takes all of these factors into consideration when determining **TRUMARKET** Prices. **GREENBOOK TRUMARKET Prices are never an absolute number.** Use them as a basis for comparison, as a point of information when considering an acquisition and as a guide when insuring for replacement value.

The "% Change in **GBTru**" is the percent change up or down (↑ ↓) in GBTru as compared to the last edition of the Guide. No change indicates just that.

All **GREENBOOK TRUMARKET PRICES** are for items in mint condition.

THE TY SWING TAGS

TY SWING TAG #1 ♥
· Single heart swing tag.

TY SWING TAG #2 ♥
· Mid 1994
· Double-sided heart swing tag opens like a book.

TY SWING TAG #3 ♥
· Mid 1995
· Double-sided heart swing tag opens like a book.
· Larger type "ty."

TY SWING TAG #4 ♥
· Mid 1996
· Double-sided heart swing tag opens like a book.
· Larger type "ty."
· "BEANIE ORIGINAL BABY" yellow star on front.
· First tag with birthday and poem.

TY SWING TAG #5 ♥
· 1998
· Double-sided heart swing tag opens like a book.
· Larger type "ty."
· "BEANIE ORIGINAL BABY" font change.

· Black and White.

· Red and White without the Beanie Baby's name.

· Red and White with the Beanie Baby's name.

· Red and White with the Beanie Baby's name.
· Clear sticker star.

· Red and White with the Beanie Baby's name.
· Printed star.

TY BEANIE BABIES CLUB

In a January 1, 1998 letter to retailers Ty announced an official Beanie Babies Club.

Details include:

- Retailers who are Official Beanie Babies Club Headquarters.
- Exclusive Membership Kits sold through these Official Beanie Babies Club Headquarters.
- Exclusive Membership Kits contain:
  Official Beanie Babies Membership Card
  Official Beanie Babies Checklist
  Official Beanie Babies Newsletter
  Official Beanie Babies Membership Certificate
  Official Beanie Babies Stickers
- A special Gift With Purchase.
- The first Gift With Purchase is an oversized, full color poster.

Mr. Warner has been quoted many times, including in this 2nd Edition Guide, as say- ing one of his goals with  Beanie Babies was to introduce children to a huge sampling of the world's animals.

Well, the adults at GREENBOOK now know more about iguanas and chameleons than we ever thought possible!

At press time there is a great deal of confusion over the new Beanies Iggy and Rainbow.

We have decided to identify the pieces consistent with the Ty Swing Tags and body tags they are shipping with because it is what the lizards should look like—iguanas have a spine, chameleons a collar. However, this is contrary to the Ty 1998 catalog and the Ty website.

If we had to guess, we'd say it was a fabric mixup.

QUIKREFERENCE-RETIRED & OUT OF PRODUCTION

RETIRED

Name	Item#	Ret.
❑ 1997 Teddy™ the holiday bear	4200	'98
❑ Ally™ the alligator	4032	'97
❑ Bessie™ the cow	4009	'97
❑ Bronty™ the brontosaurus	4085	'96
❑ Brownie™ the bear	4010	'98
❑ Bubbles™ the fish	4078	'97
❑ Bucky™ the beaver	4016	'98
❑ Bumble™ the bee	4045	'96
❑ Caw™ the crow	4071	'95
❑ Chilly™ the polar bear	4012	'95
❑ Chops™ the lamb	4019	'97
❑ Coral™ the fish	4079	'97
❑ Cubbie™ the bear	4010	'98
❑ Digger™ the crab	4027	'97
❑ Flash™ the dolphin	4021	'97
❑ Flip™ the cat	4012	'97
❑ Flutter™ the butterfly	4043	'96
❑ Garcia™ the bear	4051	'97
❑ Goldie™ the goldfish	4023	'98
❑ Grunt™ the razorback pig	4092	'97
❑ Hoot™ the owl	4073	'97
❑ Humphrey™ the camel	4060	'95
❑ Kiwi™ the toucan	4070	'97
❑ Lefty™ the donkey	4057	'97
❑ Legs™ the frog	4020	'97
❑ Libearty™ the bear	4057	'97
❑ Lizzy™ the lizard	4033	'98
❑ Magic™ the dragon	4088	'98
❑ Manny™ the manatee	4081	'97
❑ Nip™ the cat	4003	'98
❑ Peking™ the panda bear	4013	'95
❑ Radar™ the bat	4091	'97
❑ Rex™ the tyrannosaurus	4086	'96
❑ Righty™ the elephant	4086	'97
❑ Seamore™ the seal	4029	'97
❑ Slither™ the snake	4031	'95
❑ Snowball™ the snowman	4201	'98
❑ Sparky™ the Dalmatian	4100	'97
❑ Speedy™ the turtle	4030	'97
❑ Splash™ the whale	4022	'97
❑ Spook™ the ghost	4090	'98
❑ Spooky™ the ghost	4090	'98
❑ Spot™ the dog	4000	'97

RETIRED

Name	Item#	Ret.
❑ Steg™ the stegosaurus	4087	'96
❑ Sting™ the manta ray	4077	'97
❑ Tabasco™ the bull	4002	'97
❑ Tank™ the armadillo	4031	'97
❑ Teddy™ brown old face	4050	'97
❑ Teddy™ brown new face	4050	'97
❑ Teddy™ cranberry old face	4052	'95
❑ Teddy™ cranberry new face	4052	'95
❑ Teddy™ jade old face	4057	'95
❑ Teddy™ jade new face	4057	'95
❑ Teddy™ magenta old face	4056	'95
❑ Teddy™ magenta new face	4056	'95
❑ Teddy™ teal old face	4051	'95
❑ Teddy™ teal new face	4051	'95
❑ Teddy™ violet old face	4055	'95
❑ Teddy™ violet new face	4055	'95
❑ Trap™ the mouse	4042	'95
❑ Tusk™ the walrus	4076	'97
❑ Velvet™ the panther	4064	'97
❑ Web™ the spider	4041	'95

OUT OF PRODUCTION

Name	Item#
❑ Derby™ the horse ver. 1	4008
❑ Derby™ the horse ver. 2	4008
❑ Doodle™ the rooster	4171
❑ Happy™ the hippo ver. 1	4061
❑ Inch™ the inchworm ver. 1	4044
❑ Inky™ the octopus ver. 1	4028
❑ Lucky™ the ladybug ver. 1	4040
❑ Lucky™ the ladybug ver. 3	4040
❑ Mystic™ the unicorn ver. 1	4007
❑ Mystic™ the unicorn ver. 2	4007
❑ Nana™ the monkey	4067
❑ Patti™ the platypus ver. 1	4025
❑ Peanut™ the elephant ver. 1	4062
❑ Punchers™ the lobster	4026
❑ Quacker™ the duck ver. 1	4024
❑ Sly™ the fox ver. 1	4115
❑ Stripes™ the tiger ver. 1	4065
❑ Stripes™ the tiger ver. 2	4065
❑ Zip™ the cat ver. 1	4004
❑ Zip™ the cat ver. 2	4004

THE ORIGINAL 9

Name	Item#
Brownie™/Cubbie™ the bear	4010
Chocolate™ the moose	4015
Flash™ the dolphin	4021
Legs™ the frog	4020
Patti™ the platypus	4025
Punchers™/Pinchers™ the lobster	4026
Splash™ the whale	4022
Spot™ the dog	4000
Squealer™ the pig	4005

TEENIE BEANIES

Name	Item#
Patti™ the platypus	1
Pinky™ the flamingo	2
Chops™ the lamb	3
Chocolate™ the moose	4
Goldie™ the goldfish	5
Speedy™ the turtle	6
Seamore™ the seal	7
Snort™ the bull	8
Quacks™ the duck	9
Lizz™ the lizard	10

NON-USA EXCLUSIVES

Britannia™ .... Great Britain   Maple™/Pride™ .... Canada

SPECIAL EVENT EXCLUSIVES

Chicago Cubs Cubbie™ 5/18/97   Employee Christmas Bears
Chicago Cubs Cubbie™ 9/6/97   Special Olympics Maple™

BEANIES BY SUBJECT

Alligator:
☐ Ally™

Armadillo:
☐ Tank™

Bats:
☐ Batty™
☐ Radar™

Bears:
☐ 1997 Teddy™
☐ Blackie™
☐ Britannia™
☐ Brownie™
☐ Chilly™
☐ Cubbie™
☐ Curly™

Bears (cont):
☐ Garcia™
☐ Libearty™
☐ Maple™/Pride™
☐ Peace™
☐ Princess™
☐ Teddy Brown™

Bears (cont):
☐ Teddy™ Cranberry
☐ Teddy™ Jade
☐ Teddy™ Magenta
☐ Teddy™ Teal
☐ Teddy™ Violet
☐ Valentino™

Beaver:
- ☐ Bucky™

Bee:
- ☐ Bumble™

Bulls:
- ☐ Snort™
- ☐ Tabasco™

Bunnies:
- ☐ Ears™
- ☐ Floppity™
- ☐ Hippity™
- ☐ Hoppity™

Butterfly:
- ☐ Flutter™

Camel:
- ☐ Humphrey™

Cats:
- ☐ Chip™
- ☐ Flip™
- ☐ Nip™
- ☐ Pounce™
- ☐ Prance™
- ☐ Snip™
- ☐ Zip™

Chameleon:
- ☐ Rainbow™

Cows:
- ☐ Bessie™
- ☐ Daisy™

Crabs:
- ☐ Claude™
- ☐ Digger™

Crow:
- ☐ Caw™

Dinosaurs:
- ☐ Bronty™
- ☐ Rex™
- ☐ Steg™

Dogs:
- ☐ Bernie™
- ☐ Bones™
- ☐ Bruno™
- ☐ Doby™
- ☐ Dotty™
- ☐ Nanook™
- ☐ Pugsly™
- ☐ Rover™
- ☐ Scottie™
- ☐ Sparky™

Dogs (cont):
- ☐ Spot™
- ☐ Spunky™
- ☐ Tuffy™
- ☐ Weenie™
- ☐ Wrinkles™

Dolphins:
- ☐ Echo™
- ☐ Flash™

Donkey:
- ☐ Lefty™

Dragon:
- ☐ Magic™

Ducks:
- ☐ Quacker™
- ☐ Quackers™
- ☐ Quacks™

Eagle:
- ☐ Baldy™

Elephants:
- ☐ Peanut™
- ☐ Righty™

Fish:
- ☐ Bubbles™
- ☐ Coral™
- ☐ Goldie™

Flamingo:
- ☐ Pinky™

Fox:
- ☐ Sly™

Frogs:
- ☐ Legs™
- ☐ Smoochy™

Ghosts:
- ☐ Spook™
- ☐ Spooky™

Giraffe:
- ☐ Twigs™

Gorilla:
- ☐ Congo™

Hippo:
- ☐ Happy™

Horse:
- ☐ Derby™

Iguana:
- ☐ Iggy™

Inchworm:
- ☐ Inch™

Kangaroo:
- ☐ Pouch™

Koala:
- ☐ Mel™

Ladybug:
- ☐ Lucky™

Lambs:
- ☐ Chops™
- ☐ Fleece™

Leopard:
- ☐ Freckles™

Lion:
- ☐ Roary™

Lizards:
- ☐ Lizz™
- ☐ Lizzy™

Lobsters:
- ☐ Pinchers™
- ☐ Punchers™

Manatee:
- ☐ Manny™

Manta Ray:
- ☐ Sting™

Monkeys:
- ☐ Bongo™
- ☐ Nana™

Moose:
- ☐ Chocolate™

Mouse:
- ☐ Trap™

Octopus:
- ☐ Inky™

Ostrich:
- ☐ Stretch™

Otter:
- ☐ Seaweed™

Owl:
- ☐ Hoot™

Panda bear:
- ☐ Peking™

Panther:
- ☐ Velvet™

Pelican:
- ☐ Scoop™

Penguin:
- ☐ Waddle™

Pigs:
- ☐ Grunt™
- ☐ Squealer™

Platypus:
- ☐ Patti™

Puffin:
- ☐ Puffer™

Raccoon:
- ☐ Ringo™

Rhino:
- ☐ Spike™

Roosters:
- ☐ Doodle™
- ☐ Strut™

Seal:
- ☐ Seamore™

Shark:
- ☐ Crunch™

Skunk:
- ☐ Stinky™

Snakes:
- ☐ Hissy™
- ☐ Slither™

Snowman:
- ☐ Snowball™

Spiders:
- ☐ Spinner™
- ☐ Web™

Squirrel:
- ☐ Nuts™

Swan:
- ☐ Gracie™

Tigers:
- ☐ Blizzard™
- ☐ Stripes™

Toucan:
- ☐ Kiwi™

Turkey:
- ☐ Gobbles™

Turtle:
- ☐ Speedy™

Unicorn:
- ☐ Mystic™

Walrus:
- ☐ Jolly™
- ☐ Tusk™

Whales:
- ☐ Splash™
- ☐ Waves™

Zebra:
- ☐ Ziggy™

QUIKREFERENCE-BEANIE BABIES BIRTHDAYS

JANUARY
Jan. 3, 1993	Spot™
Jan. 6, 1993	Patti™
Jan. 13, 1996	Crunch™
Jan. 14, 1997	Spunky™
Jan. 15, 1996	Mel™
Jan. 18, 1994	Bones™
Jan. 21, 1996	Nuts™
Jan. 25, 1995	Peanut™
Jan. 26, 1996	Chip™

FEBRUARY
Feb. 1, 1996	Peace™
Feb. 13, 1995	Stinky™
Feb. 13, 1995	Pinky™
Feb. 14, 1994	Valentino™
Feb. 17, 1996	Baldy™
Feb. 20, 1996	Roary™
Feb. 22, 1995	Tank™
Feb. 25, 1994	Happy™
Feb. 27, 1996	Sparky™
Feb. 28, 1995	Flip™

MARCH
Mar. 2, 1995	Coral™
Mar. 6, 1994	Nip™
Mar. 8, 1996	Doodle™
Mar. 8, 1996	Strut™
Mar. 14, 1994	Ally™
Mar. 19, 1996	Seaweed™
Mar. 21, 1996	Fleece™
Mar. 28, 1994	Zip™

APRIL
Apr. 3, 1996	Hoppity™
Apr. 4, 1997	Hissy™
Apr. 12, 1996	Curly™
Apr. 18, 1995	Ears™
Apr. 19, 1994	Quackers™
Apr. 23, 1993	Squealer™
Apr. 25, 1993	Legs™
Apr. 27, 1993	Chocolate™

MAY
May. 1, 1995	Lucky™
May. 1, 1996	Wrinkles™
May. 2, 1996	Pugsly™
May. 3, 1996	Chops™
May. 10, 1994	Daisy™
May. 11, 1995	Lizzy™
May. 13, 1993	Flash™
May. 15, 1995	Tabasco™
May. 15, 1995	Snort™
May. 19, 1995	Twigs™
May. 21, 1994	Mystic™
May. 28, 1996	Floppity™
May. 30, 1996	Rover™

JUNE
Jun. 1, 1996	Hippity™
Jun. 3, 1996	Freckles™
Jun. 8, 1995	Bucky™
Jun. 8, 1995	Manny™
Jun. 11, 1995	Stripes™
Jun. 15, 1996	Scottie™
Jun. 17, 1996	Gracie™
Jun. 19, 1993	Pinchers™
Jun. 27, 1995	Bessie™

JULY
Jul. 1, 1996	Scoop™
Jul. 1, 1996	Maple™
Jul. 2, 1995	Bubbles™
Jul. 4, 1996	Libearty™
Jul. 4, 1996	Lefty™
Jul. 4, 1996	Righty™
Jul. 8, 1993	Splash™
Jul. 14, 1995	Ringo™
Jul. 15, 1994	Blackie™
Jul. 19, 1995	Grunt™
Jul. 20, 1995	Weenie™

AUGUST
Aug. 1, 1995	Garcia™
Aug. 9, 1995	Hoot™
Aug. 12, 1997	Iggy™
Aug. 13, 1996	Spike™
Aug. 14, 1994	Speedy™
Aug. 17, 1995	Bongo™
Aug. 23, 1995	Digger™
Aug. 27, 1995	Sting™
Aug. 28, 1997	Pounce™

SEPTEMBER
Sep. 3, 1995	Inch™
Sep. 3, 1996	Claude™
Sep. 5, 1995	Magic™
Sep. 9, 1997	Bruno™
Sep. 12, 1996	Sly™
Sep. 16, 1995	Kiwi™
Sep. 16, 1995	Derby™
Sep. 18, 1995	Tusk™
Sep. 21, 1997	Stretch™

OCTOBER
Oct. 1, 1997	Smoochy™
Oct. 3, 1996	Bernie™
Oct. 9, 1996	Doby™
Oct. 12, 1996	Tuffy™
Oct. 14, 1997	Rainbow™
Oct. 16, 1995	Bumble™
Oct. 17, 1996	Dotty™
Oct. 22, 1996	Snip™
Oct. 28, 1996	Spinner™
Oct. 29, 1996	Batty™
Oct. 30, 1995	Radar™
Oct. 31, 1995	Spooky™

NOVEMBER
Nov. 3, 1997	Puffer™
Nov. 6, 1996	Pouch™
Nov. 9, 1996	Congo™
Nov. 14, 1993	Cubbie™
Nov. 14, 1994	Goldie™
Nov. 20, 1997	Prance™
Nov. 21, 1996	Nanook™
Nov. 27, 1996	Gobbles™
Nov. 28, 1995	Teddy™ Brown
Nov. 29, 1994	Inky™

DECEMBER
Dec. 2, 1996	Jolly™
Dec. 8, 1996	Waves™
Dec. 12, 1996	Blizzard™
Dec. 14, 1996	Seamore™
Dec. 16, 1995	Velvet™
Dec. 19, 1995	Waddle™
Dec. 21, 1996	Echo™
Dec. 22, 1996	Snowball™
Dec. 24, 1995	Ziggy™
Dec. 25, 1996 1997	Teddy™

1997 TEDDY™

Issued: 10/1/97

Status: Retired 1/1/98

Description: Bear in red and white
Santa hat and matching scarf.

Birthday: 12/25/96

Poem:

Beanie Babies are special no doubt
All filled with love—inside and out
Wishes for fun times filled with joy
Ty's holiday teddy is a magical toy!

GBTru: $50   **Item # 4200**

Bought ___/___/___   for $_____.

ALLY™

Issued: 1994

Status: Retired 10/1/97

Description: Green and brown
alligator.

Birthday: 3/14/94

Poem:

When Ally gets out of classes
He wears a hat and dark glasses
He plays bass in a street band
He's the coolest gator in the land!

GBTru: $25 ↑400%   **Item # 4032**

'97
$5

Bought ___/___/___   for $_____.

BALDY™

Issued: 5/11/97

Status: Current

Description: Eagle.

Birthday: 2/17/96

Poem:

Hair on his head is quite scant
We suggest Baldy get a transplant
Watching over the land of the free
Hair in his eyes would make it hard
to see!

GBTru: $5 no change   **Item # 4074**

'97
$5

Bought ___/___/___   for $_____.

B is for Batty...

BATTY™

GBTru: $5   Item # 4105

Issued: 10/1/97
Status: Current
Description: Rose-beige bat with velcro tabs on lower wings so they can fold.
Birthday: 10/29/96
Poem:

Bats may make some people jitter
Please don't be scared of this critter
If you're lonely or have nothing to do
This Beanie Baby would love to hug you!

Bought ___/___/___ for $_____.

BERNIE™

GBTru: $5 no change   Item # 4109

'97
$5

Issued: 1/1/97
Status: Current
Description: Tan, cream and brown tricolor St. Bernard dog.
Birthday: 10/3/96
Poem:

This little dog can't wait to grow
To rescue people lost in snow
Don't let him out—keep him on your shelf
He doesn't know how to rescue himself!

Bought ___/___/___ for $_____.

BESSIE™

GBTru: $35 ↑600%   Item # 4009

'97
$5

Issued: 1995
Status: Retired 10/1/97
Description: Brown and white cow.
Birthday: 6/27/95
Poem:

Bessie the cow likes to dance and sing
Because music is her favorite thing
Every night when you're counting sheep
She'll sing you a song to put you to sleep.

Bought ___/___/___ for $_____.

BLACKIE™

Issued: 1994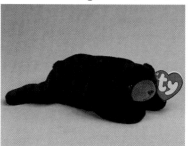

Status: Current

Description: Black bear.

Birthday: 7/15/94

Poem:

Living in a national park
He only played after dark
Then he met his friend Cubbie
Now they play when it's sunny!

GBTru: $5 no change   Item # 4011

'97
$5

Bought ___ / ___ / ___ for $_____.

BLIZZARD™

Issued: 5/11/97

Status: Current

Description: Black and white Snow Tiger.

Birthday: 12/12/96

Poem:

In the mountains, where it's snowy and cold
Lives a beautiful tiger, I've been told
Black and white, she's hard to compare
Of all the tigers, she is most rare.

GBTru: $5 no change   Item # 4163

'97
$5

Bought ___ / ___ / ___ for $_____.

BONES™

Issued: 1995

Status: Current

Description: Brown dog.

Birthday: 1/18/94

Poem:

Bones is a dog that loves to chew
Chairs and a table and a smelly old shoe
"You're so destructive" all would shout
But that all stopped, when his teeth fell out!

GBTru: $5 no change   Item # 4001

'97
$5

Bought ___ / ___ / ___ for $_____.

21

B is for Bongo...

BONGO™

GBTru: $5 no change   Item # 4067

'97
$5

Issued: 1995
Status: Current
Description: Brown monkey. Tail color has changed back and forth between tan and brown. Tan is a little harder to find. "Nana" was the original Bongo. See page 48.
Birthday: 8/17/95
Poem: Bongo the monkey lives in a tree
He's the happiest monkey that you'll ever see
In his spare time he plays the guitar
One of these days he will be a big star!

Bought _____ / _____ / _____ for $_____.

BRITANNIA™

GBTru: NE   Item # 4601

Issued: 1/1/98
Status: European Exclusive
Description: Ty Europe Exclusive bear has British flag on chest and red ribbon around neck.
Birthday: N/A at press time
Poem: N/A at press time

(N/A = Not Available
  NE = Not Established)

Bought _____ / _____ / _____ for $_____.

BRONTY™

GBTru: $500 ↑33%   Item # 4085

'97
$375

Issued: 1995
Status: Retired 1996
Description: Blue tie-dye Brontosaurus.
Birthday: unknown
Poem: None.

Bought _____ / _____ / _____ for $_____.

BROWNIE™

Issued: 1993 💙

Status: Retired 1/1/98

Description: Brown bear. One of the "Original 9." Available under this name for very short time. Name changed to Cubbie in 1994. See Cubbie on page 27. IMPORTANT: All Brownies have the single Ty Heart Swing Tag #1 with the name "Brownie."

Birthday: unknown

Poem: None.

Bought ___/___/___ for $_____.

GBTru: $1800 ↑800%   Item # 4010

'97
$200

BRUNO™

Issued: 1/1/98 🖐

Status: Current

Description: Terrier. Brown blanket color pattern w/white muzzle, paws and underside.

Birthday: 9/9/97

Poem:

Bruno the dog thinks he's a brute
But all the other Beanies think he's cute
He growls at his tail and runs in a ring
And everyone says, "Oh, how darling!"

Bought ___/___/___ for $_____.

GBTru: $5   Item # 4183

BUBBLES™

Issued: 1995 💙 💙

Status: Retired 5/11/97

Description: Black and yellow fish.

Birthday: 7/2/95

Poem:

All day long Bubbles likes to swim
She never gets tired of flapping her fins
Bubbles lived in a sea of blue
Now she is ready to come home with you!

Bought ___/___/___ for $_____.

GBTru: $70 ↑100%   Item # 4078

'97
$35

23

B is for Bucky...

BUCKY™

GBTru: $25 ↑400%   Item # 4016

'97
$5

Issued: 1995 ③ ④ ⑤
Status: Retired 1/1/98
Description: Brown beaver.
Birthday: 6/8/95
Poem:
His teeth are as shiny as can be
Often used for cutting trees
He hides in his dam night and day
Maybe for you he will come out and
play!

Bought ___/___/___ for $_____.

BUMBLE™

GBTru: $325 ↑117%   Item # 4045

'97
$150

Issued: 1995 ③ ④
Status: Retired 1996
Description: Yellow & black bee. Ty
Heart Swing Tag #4 w/poem and
birthday is harder to find than
older #3 Swing Tag. Add $100 for
the #4 Swing Tag.
Birthday: 10/16/95
Poem: Bumble the bee will not sting you
It is only love that this bee will bring you
So don't be afraid to give this bee a hug
Because Bumble the bee is a love-bug.

Bought ___/___/___ for $_____.

CAW™

GBTru: $350 ↑133%   Item # 4071

'97
$150

Issued: 1995 ③
Status: Retired 1995
Description: Black crow.
Birthday: unknown
Poem: None.

Bought ___/___/___ for $_____.

C is for Chilly...

CHILLY™

Issued: 1994 ❤ ❤ ❤

Status: Retired 1995

Description: White polar bear.

Birthday: unknown

Poem: None.

GBTru: $950 ↑27%   Item # 4012

'97
$750

Bought ___/___/___ for $_____.

CHIP™

Issued: 5/11/97 ❤ ❤

Status: Current

Description: Brown, black and white Calico cat with pink nose.

Birthday: 1/26/96

Poem:

Black and gold, brown and white
The shades of her coat are quite a sight
At mixing her colors she was a master
On anyone else it would be a disaster!

GBTru: $5 no change   Item # 4121

'97
$5

Bought ___/___/___ for $_____.

CHOCOLATE™

Issued: 1994 ❤ ❤ ❤ ❤ ❤

Status: Current

Description: Brown moose with orange antlers. One of the "Original 9." Also exists as a TBB.

Birthday: 4/27/93

Poem:

Licorice, gum and peppermint candy
This moose always has these handy
But there is one more thing he likes to eat
Can you guess his favorite sweet?

GBTru: $5 no change   Item # 4015

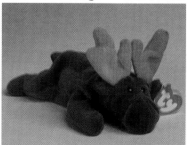

'97
$5

Bought ___/___/___ for $_____.

C is for Chops...

CHOPS™

GBTru: $95 ↑27%   Item # 4019

'97
$75

Issued: 1996 ③ ④
Status: Retired 1/1/97
Description: Cream lamb with black face and inner ears. Also exists as a TBB.
Birthday: 5/3/96
Poem:
Chops is a little lamb
This lamb you'll surely know
Because every path that you may take
This lamb is sure to go!

Bought ___/___/___ for $_____

CLAUDE™

GBTru: $5 no change   Item # 4083

'97
$5

Issued: 5/11/97 ④ ⑤
Status: Current
Description: Tie-dye crab.
Birthday: 9/3/96
Poem:
Claude the crab paints by the sea
A famous artist he hopes to be
But the tide came in and his paints fell
Now his art is on his shell!

Bought ___/___/___ for $_____

CONGO™

GBTru: $5 no change   Item # 4160

'97
$5

Issued: 1996 ④ ⑤
Status: Current
Description: Black gorilla.
Birthday: 11/9/96
Poem:
Black as night and fierce is he
On the ground or in a tree
Strong and mighty as the Congo
He's related to our friend Bongo!

Bought ___/___/___ for $_____

CORAL™

Issued: 1995
Status: Retired 1/1/97
Description: Tie-dye tropical fish.
Birthday: 3/2/95
Poem:
Coral is beautiful, as you know
Made of colors in the rainbow
Whether it's pink, yellow or blue
These colors were chosen just for you!

GBTru: $75 ↑50%   **Item # 4079**

'97
$50

Bought ___ / ___ / ___ for $_____.

CRUNCH™

Issued: 1/1/97
Status: Current
Description: Shark with blue-grey body and white belly.
Birthday: 1/13/96
Poem:
What's for breakfast? What's for lunch?
Yum? Delicious! Munch, munch, munch!
He's eating everything by the bunch
That's the reason we named him Crunch!

GBTru: $5 no change   **Item # 4130**

'97
$5

Bought ___ / ___ / ___ for $_____.

CUBBIE™

Issued: 1994
Status: Retired 1/1/98
Description: Brown bear. One of the "Original 9." Original name "Brownie." See page 23. Name changed to Cubbie in 1994. See Special Cubs Cubbies page 85.
Birthday: 11/14/93
Poem:
Cubbie used to eat crackers and honey
And what happened to him was funny
He was stung by fourteen bees
Now Cubbie eats broccoli and cheese.

GBTru: $50 ↑900%   **Item # 4010**

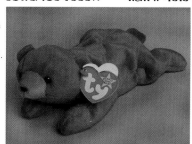

'97
$5

Bought ___ / ___ / ___ for $_____.

27

C is for Curly...

CURLY™

GBTru: $5 no change   Item # 4052

'97
$5

Issued: 1996

Status: Current

Description: Brown bear with burgundy ribbon, curly-textured fabric.

Birthday: 4/12/96

Poem:
A bear so cute with hair that's curly
You will love and want him surely
To this bear always be true
He will be a friend to you!

Bought ___/___/___ for $_____.

DAISY™

GBTru: $5 no change   Item # 4006

'97
$5

Issued: 1994

Status: Current

Description: Black and white Holstein cow.

Birthday: 5/10/94

Poem:
Daisy drinks milk each night
So her coat is shiny and bright
Milk is good for your hair and skin
What a way for your day to begin!

Bought ___/___/___ for $_____.

10-8-97

Dear Company,
I my name is Andrea
I have brown hair & brown eyes.
I'm kind. I'm pretty & beautiful.
I'm writing to you because
I want you to send me a letter
telling me what one's are retired,
which ones are coming out
soon.

Your Friend,
Andrea

P.S. Don't forget!

*UTTM = Up To The Minute

Throughout the life of this Second Edition we'll do our best to keep your Guide current. If you'd like an UTTM* Bookmark Update when available, please send a #10 self-addressed, stamped envelope with "BB Update" written on the outside lower left corner to:

GREENBOOK - BB Update
PO Box 645
Pacific Grove, CA 93950

We'll hold your envelope until there's news & then send out the Update. (Note: Updates stop upon publication of the next edition.)

DERBY™ VERSION 1

Issued: 1995 🛡️
Status: Out Of Production 1995
Description: All brown horse with dark brown mane and tail.
Version 1: <u>Soft fine yarn</u> for mane and tail. Change to Version 2 in 1995.
Birthday: unknown
Poem: None.

GBTru: $900 ↑500%   **Item # 4008**

'97
$150

Bought ____/____/____ for $_____.

DERBY™ VERSION 2

Issued: 1995 🛡️ 🛡️
Status: Out Of Production 1998
Description: All brown horse with dark brown mane and tail. Version 2: <u>Coarse yarn</u> for mane and tail. Change to Version 3 in 1998.
Birthday: 9/16/95
Poem:
All the other horses used to tattle
Because Derby never wore his saddle
He left the stables, and the horses too
Just so Derby can be with you!

GBTru: $15 ↑200%   **Item # 4008**

'97
$5

Bought ____/____/____ for $*20.00*

DERBY™ VERSION 3

Issued: 1998 🛡️
Status: Current
Description: Horse. Version 3: Brown horse with white star.
Birthday: 9/16/95
Poem:
All the other horses used to tattle
Because Derby never wore his saddle
He left the stables, and the horses too
Just so Derby can be with you!

GBTru: $5   **Item # 4008**

Bought ____/____/____ for $*6.00*

D is for Digger...

DIGGER™ VERSION 1

GBTru: $375 ↑25%   Item # 4027

'97
$300

Issued: 1995 ② ③
Status: Retired 5/11/97
Description: Crab. Version 1: Orange crab. Change to Version 2 in 1995.
Birthday: unknown
Poem: None.

Bought ___/___/___ for $_____.

DIGGER™ VERSION 2

GBTru: $50 ↑67%   Item # 4027

'97
$30

Issued: 1995 ③ ④
Status: Retired 5/11/97
Description: Crab. Version 2: Red crab.
Birthday: 8/23/95
Poem:
Digging in the sand and walking sideways
That's how Digger spends her days
Hard on the outside but sweet deep inside
Basking in the sun, riding the tide!

Bought ___/___/___ for $_____.

DOBY™

GBTru: $5 no change   Item # 4110

'97
$5

Issued: 1/1/97 ④ ⑤
Status: Current
Description: Brown and black Doberman dog.
Birthday: 10/9/96
Poem:
This dog is little but he has might
Keep him close when you sleep at night
He lays around with nothing to do
Until he sees it's time to protect you!

Bought ___/___/___ for $_____.

DOODLE™

Issued: 5/11/97

Status: Out Of Production 8/97

GBTru: $40 ↑700%   **Item # 4171**

Description: Rooster. Red crest, wings and tail on soft yellow tie-dye body. Name changed to Strut in 8/97. See page 69.

Birthday: 3/8/96

Poem:

Listen closely to "Cock-a-doodle-doo"
What's the rooster saying to you?
Hurry, wake up sleepy head
We have lots to do, get out of bed!

Bought ___/___/___ for $_____.

'97
$5

DOTTY™

Issued: 5/11/97

Status: Current

GBTru: $5 no change   **Item # 4100**

Description: Dalmatian. Black ears on spotted dog.

Birthday: 10/17/96

Poem:

The Beanies all thought it was a big joke
While writing her tag, their ink pen broke
She got in the way, and got all spotty
So now the Beanies call her Dotty!

Bought ___/___/___ for $_____.

'97
$5

EARS™

Issued: 1996

Status: Current

GBTru: $5 no change   **Item # 4018**

Description: Brown bunny.

Birthday: 4/18/95

Poem:

He's been eating carrots so long
Didn't understand what was wrong
Couldn't see the board during classes
Until the doctor gave him glasses!

Bought ___/___/___ for $_____.

'97
$5

E is for Echo...

ECHO™

GBTru: $5 no change   Item # 4180

'97
$5

Issued: 5/11/97 ④ ⑤
Status: Current
Description: Dolphin. Echo and Waves were originally shipped with each others swing tag and body tag. See page 67.
Birthday: 12/21/96
Poem:
Echo the dolphin lives in the sea
Playing with her friends, like you and me
Through the waves she echoes the sound
"I'm so glad to have you around!"

Bought ___/___/___ for $_____.

FLASH™

GBTru: $65 ↑86%   Item # 4021

'97
$35

Issued: 1994 ① ② ③ ④
Status: Retired 5/11/97
Description: Grey dolphin. One of the "Original 9."
Birthday: 5/13/93
Poem:
You know dolphins are the smartest breed
Well Flash the dolphin knows how to read
She's teaching her friend Splash to read too
So maybe one day they can both read to you.

Alternate Poem:
You know dolphins are a smart breed
Our friend Flash knows how to read
Splash the whale is the one who taught her
Although reading is difficult under the water!

Bought ___/___/___ for $_____.

FLEECE™

Issued: 1/1/97 4️ 5️
Status: Current
Description: White lamb with curly-textured fabric.
Birthday: 3/21/96
Poem:

Fleece would like to sing a lullaby
Please be patient, she's really shy
When you sleep, keep her by your ear
Her song will leave you nothing to fear.

GBTru: $5 no change   Item # 4125

'97
$5

Bought ___/___/___ for $_____.

FLIP™

Issued: 1996 3️ 4️
Status: Retired 10/1/97
Description: White cat with pink whiskers, nose and inner ears, blue eyes.
Birthday: 2/28/95
Poem:

Flip the cat is an acrobat
She loves playing on her mat
This cat flips with such grace and flair
She can somersault in midair.

GBTru: $45 ↑800%   Item # 4012

'97
$5

Bought ___/___/___ for $_____.

FLOPPITY™

Issued: 1/1/97 4️ 5️
Status: Current
Description: Lavender bunny.
Birthday: 5/28/96
Poem:

Floppity hops from here to there
Searching for eggs without a care
Lavender coat from head to toe
All dressed up and nowhere to go!

GBTru: $5 no change   Item # 4118

'97
$5

Bought ___/___/___ for $_____.

F is for Flutter...

FLUTTER™

GBTru: **$500 ↑43%**   Item # 4043

'97
$350

Issued: 1995 🛡2 🛡3
Status: Retired 1996
Description: Tie-dye butterfly.
Birthday: unknown
Poem: None.

Bought ___/___/___   for $_____

FRECKLES™

GBTru: **$5 no change**   Item # 4066

'97
$5

Issued: 1996 🛡4 🛡5
Status: Current
Description: Leopard.
Birthday: 6/3/96
Poem:
From the trees he hunts his prey
In the night and in the day
He's the king of camouflage
Look real close, he's no mirage!

Bought ___/___/___   for $_____

GARCIA™

GBTru: **$100 ↑100%**   Item # 4051

'97
$50

Issued: 1995 🛡3 🛡4
Status: Retired 5/11/97
Description: Multicolored tie-dye bear.
Birthday: 8/1/95
Poem:
The Beanies use to follow him around
Because Garcia traveled from town to town
He's pretty popular as you can see
Some even say he's legendary.

Bought ___/___/___   for $_____

G is for Gobbles...

GOBBLES™

Issued: 10/1/97

Status: Current

GBTru: $5   Item # 4034

Description: Turkey. Brown body with brown and red wings. The bill and feet are yellow and the head is red. The tail is circles of brown, red & white.

Birthday: 11/27/96

Poem: Gobbles the turkey loves to eat
Once a year she has a feast
I have a secret I'd like to divulge
If she eats too much her tummy will bulge!

Bought ___/___/___ for $_____.

GOLDIE™

Issued: 1994

GBTru: $50 ↑900%   Item # 4023

Status: Retired 1/1/98

Description: Goldfish. Also exists as a TBB.

Birthday: 11/14/94

Poem:
She's got the rhythm, she's got the soul
What more could you want in a fish bowl?
Through sound waves Goldie swam
Because this goldfish likes to jam.

Bought ___/___/___ for $_____.

'97
$5

GRACIE™

Issued: 1/1/97

GBTru: $5 no change   Item # 4126

Status: Current

Description: White swan.

Birthday: 6/17/96

Poem:
As a duckling, she was confused,
Birds on the lake were quite amused.
Poking fun until she would cry,
Now the most beautiful swan at Ty!

Bought ___/___/___ for $_____.

'97
$5

G is for Grunt...

GRUNT™

GBTru: $125 ↑257%   Item # 4092

'97
$35

Issued: 1995
Status: Retired 5/11/97
Description: Red razorback pig.
Birthday: 7/19/95
Poem:
Some Beanies think Grunt is tough
No surprise, he's scary enough
But if you take him home you'll see
Grunt is the sweetest Beanie Baby!

Bought ___/___/___ for $_____.

HAPPY™ VERSION 1

GBTru: $350 ↑17%   Item # 4061

'97
$300

Issued: 1994
Status: Out Of Production 1995
Description: Hippo. Version 1: Light grey. Change to Version 2 in 1995.
Birthday: unknown
Poem: None.

Bought ___/___/___ for $_____.

HAPPY™ VERSION 2

GBTru: $5 no change   Item # 4061

'97
$5

Issued: 1995
Status: Current
Description: Hippo. Version 2: Lavender.
Birthday: 2/25/94
Poem:
Happy the hippo loves to wade
In the river and in the shade
When Happy shoots water out of his snout
You'll know he's happy without a doubt!

Bought ___/___/___ for $_____.

HIPPITY™

Issued: 1/1/97 ④ ⑤
Status: Current
Description: Mint green bunny.
Birthday: 6/1/96
Poem:

Hippity is a cute little bunny
Dressed in green, he looks quite funny
Twitching his nose in the air
Sniffing a flower here and there!

GBTru: $5 no change   Item # 4119

'97
$5

Bought ___/___/___ for $_____.

HISSY™

Issued: 1/1/98 ⑤
Status: Current
Description: Snake has gray upper
body and lemony yellow underside.
Birthday: 4/4/97
Poem:

Curled and coiled and ready to play
He waits for you patiently every day
He'll keep his best friend, but not his skin
And stay with you through thick and
thin!

GBTru: $5   Item # 4185

Bought ___/___/___ for $_____.

HOOT™

Issued: 1995 ③ ④
Status: Retired 10/1/97
Description: Owl.
Birthday: 8/9/95
Poem:

Late to bed, late to rise
Nevertheless, Hoot's quite wise
Studies by candlelight, nothing new
Like a president, do you know who?

GBTru: $35 ↑600%   Item # 4073

'97
$5

Bought ___/___/___ for $_____.

H is for Hoppity...

HOPPITY™

GBTru: $5 no change   Item # 4117

'97
$5

Issued: 1/1/97 ④ ⑤
Status: Current
Description: Pink bunny.
Birthday: 4/3/96
Poem:
Hopscotch is what she likes to play
If you don't join in, she'll hop away
So play a game if you have the time,
She likes to play, rain or shine.

Bought ___/___/___ for $_____.

HUMPHREY™

GBTru: $1100 ↑83%   Item # 4060

'97
$600

Issued: 1994 ① ② ③
Status: Retired 1995
Description: Brown camel.
Birthday: unknown
Poem: None.

Bought ___/___/___ for $_____.

IGGY™

GBTru: $5   Item # 4038

Issued: 1/1/98 ⑤
Status: Current
Description: Tie-dye iguana w/
prominent eyes and spiny body
trim.
Birthday: 8/12/97
Poem:
Sitting on a rock, basking in the sun
Is this Iguana's idea of fun
Towel and glasses, book and beach
chair
His life is so perfect without a care!

Bought ___/___/___ for $_____.

I is for Inch...

INCH™ VERSION 1

Issued: 1995 💗 💗

Status: Out Of Production 1996

GBTru: $100 no change   Item # 4044

Description: Multi-colored inchworm.
Version 1: Black <u>felt</u> antenna. Change
to Version 2 in 1996.

Birthday: 9/3/95

Poem:

Inch the worm is a friend of mine
He goes so slow all the time
Inching around from here to there
Traveling the world without a care.

'97
$100

Bought ___ / ___ / ___ for $_____.

INCH™ VERSION 2

Issued: 1996 💗 💗

Status: Current

GBTru: $5 no change   Item # 4044

Description: Multi-colored inchworm.
Version 2: Black <u>yarn</u> antenna.

Birthday: 9/3/95

Poem:

Inch the worm is a friend of mine
He goes so slow all the time
Inching around from here to there
Traveling the world without a care.

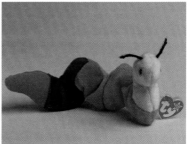

'97
$5

Bought ___ / ___ / ___ for $_____.

Brooke from Florida
wrote a nice note telling
us how much she liked
the GREENBOOK. She
had a suggestion that we
rate each Beanie on this
scale of 1- 10:

And then in the begginning of the
book you could put this.

1. I Hate it
2. I think one part of it's cute
3. It's lookable
4. It's okay?
5. nice
6. Good + nice
7. Great + Super
8. Fantastic
9. Exellent
10. Exellently Outrageously superly
   duperly cool + cute

I is for Inky...

INKY™ VERSION 1

GBTru: $350 ↑56%   Item # 4028

'97
$225

Issued: 1994 ❶ ❷ ❸
Status: Out Of Production 1995
Description: Octopus. Version 1: Tan.
Some had no mouth. Change to
Version 2 in 1995.
Birthday: unknown
Poem: None.

Bought ____/____/____ for $_____.

INKY™ VERSION 2

GBTru: $5 no change   Item # 4028

'97
$5

Issued: 1995 ❸ ❹ ❺
Status: Current
Description: Octopus. Version 2:
Pink.
Birthday: 11/29/94
Poem:
Inky's head is big and round
As he swims he makes no sound
If you need a hand, don't hesitate
Inky can help because he has eight!

Bought ____/____/____ for $_____.

JOLLY™

GBTru: $5 no change   Item # 4082

'97
$5

Issued: 5/11/97 ❹ ❺
Status: Current
Description: Walrus.
Birthday: 12/2/96
Poem:
Jolly the walrus is not very serious
He laughs and laughs until he's
delirious
He often reminds me of my dad
Always happy, never sad!

Bought ____/____/____ for $_____.

KIWI™

Issued: 1995
Status: Retired 1/1/97
Description: Toucan. Black with multi-colored bill.
Birthday: 9/16/95
Poem:
Kiwi waits for the April showers
Watching a garden bloom with flowers
There trees grow with fruit that's sweet
I'm sure you'll guess his favorite treat!

GBTru: $90 ↑80%   Item # 4070

'97
$50

Bought ___/___/___ for $_____.

LEFTY™

Issued: 1996
Status: Retired 1/1/97
Description: Blue donkey with American flag is symbol of the Democratic Party.
Birthday: 7/4/96
Poem: Donkeys to the left, elephants to the right
Often seems like a crazy sight
This whole game seems very funny
Until you realize they're spending your money!

GBTru: $135 ↑170%   Item # 4057

'97
$50

Bought ___/___/___ for $_____.

LEGS™

Issued: 1993
Status: Retired 10/1/97
Description: Green frog. One of the "Original 9."
Birthday: 4/25/93
Poem:
Legs lives in a hollow log
Legs likes to play leap frog
If you like to hang out at the lake
Legs will be the new friend you make!

GBTru: $25 ↑400%   Item # 4020

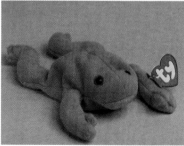

'97
$5

Bought ___/___/___ for $_____.

41

L is for Libearty...

LIBEARTY™

GBTru: $150 ↑200%   Item # 4057

'97
$50

Issued: 1996 🛡
Status: Retired 1/1/97
Description: White bear with American flag on chest and red and blue ribbon around neck was introduced to commemorate the 1996 Olympics.
Birthday: 7/4/96
Poem: I am called Libearty
I wear the flag for all to see
Hope and freedom is my way
That's why I wear flag USA.

Bought ___/___/___ for $_____.

These are some ideas for some new Beanie babies. I have worked verry hard on drawing my ideas for you. I have 89 of them. If you can make them will you pleasse send me one of **each**

yours
truly,
Julie

Birthday Bear
Jan. 22, 1997

GREENBOOK estimates the Ty Creative & Product Development Staff to be in the thousands ranging in age from 5 to 95.

LIZZY™ VERSION 1

Issued: 1995 ② ③

Status: Retired 1/1/98

Description: Lizard.
Version 1: Tie-dye. Change to
Version 2 in 1996.

Birthday: unknown

Poem: None.

GBTru: $500 ↑43%   Item # 4033

'97
$350

Bought ___ / ___ / ___ for $_____.

LIZZY™ VERSION 2

Issued: 1996 ③ ④ ⑤

Status: Retired 1/1/98

Description: Lizard. Version 2: Blue
back w/black design, shaded yellow
underside. Also exists as TBB, "Lizz."

Birthday: 5/11/95

Poem:
Her best friend Legs was at her house
waiting
Today is the day they go roller
blading
But Lizzy Lou had to stay home
So Legs had to roller blade alone.

GBTru: $35 ↑600%   Item # 4033

'97
$5

With stacks of mail like this note from
Susan in Iowa, we very quickly became
aware of the fact that Lizzy had another
poem!

Alternate Poem:
Lizzy loves Legs the frog
She hides with him under logs
Both of them search for flies
Underneath the clear blue skies!

Dear Sir,
My daughter has a version 2 of
Lizzy the lizard with a different poem
on its tag then appears in your greenbook.
My daughters poem reads:
Lizzy loves Legs the frog
She hides with him under logs
Both of them search for flies
Underneath the clear blue skies!
I was wondering if this was just a
misprint in your book or not.
Thank you for your help in this
matter.

Susan

Bought ___ / ___ / ___ for $_____.

L is for Lucky...

LUCKY™ VERSION 1

GBTru: $100 no change   Item # 4040

'97
$100

Issued: 1994 ❶ ❷ ❸
Status: Out Of Production 1996
Description: Ladybug. Version 1:
Seven black felt spots glued on.
Change to Version 2 Summer
1996.
Birthday: unknown
Poem: None.

Bought ___/___/___ for $_____.

LUCKY™ VERSION 2

GBTru: $5 no change   Item # 4040

'97
$5

Issued: 1996 ❹ ❺
Status: Current
Description: Ladybug. Version 2:
Approximately 11 black spots are part of
fabric. (Can be +/- 3 depending on how it's
sewn.) Introduced Summer 1996 and
Version 2 is in current production.
Birthday: 5/1/95
Poem: Lucky the lady bug loves the lotto
"Someone must win" that's her motto
But save your dimes and even a penny
Don't spend on the lotto and
You'll have many!

Bought ___/___/___ for $_____.

LUCKY™ VERSION 3

GBTru: $400 ↑7900% Item # 4040

'97
$5

Issued: 1996 ❹
Status: Out Of Production 1996
Description: Ladybug. Version 3:
Approximately 21 small spots are part of
fabric. (Can be +/- 3 depending on how it's
sewn.) Introduced late 1996. Current
production has returned to Version 2.
Birthday: 5/1/95
Poem: Lucky the lady bug loves the lotto
"Someone must win" that's her motto
But save your dimes and even a penny
Don't spend on the lotto and
You'll have many!

Bought ___/___/___ for $_____.

M is for Magic...

MAGIC™ VERSION 1

Issued: 1995 🛡️ 🛡️
Status: Retired 1/1/98

GBTru: $50 ↑900%   Item # 4088

Description: White dragon with iridescent wings and scales down back. Version 1: Wing thread color was <u>pale pink</u>.

Birthday: 9/5/95

Poem:

Magic the dragon lives in a dream
The most beautiful that you have ever seen
Through magic lands she likes to fly
Look up and watch her, way up high!

Bought ___/___/___ for $_____.

'97
$5

MAGIC™ VERSION 2

Issued: 1996 🛡️
Status: Retired 1/1/98

GBTru: $150 ↑100%   Item # 4088

Description: White dragon with iridescent wings and scales down back. Version 2: Wing thread color was <u>hot pink</u>.

Birthday: 9/5/95

Poem: Magic the dragon lives in a dream
The most beautiful that you have ever seen
Through magic lands she likes to fly
Look up and watch her, way up high!

Bought ___/___/___ for $_____.

'97
$75

MANNY™

Issued: 1995 🛡️ 🛡️
Status: Retired 5/11/97

GBTru: $85 ↑143%   Item # 4081

Description: Grey manatee.

Birthday: 6/8/95

Poem:

Manny is sometimes called a sea cow
She likes to twirl and likes to bow
Manny sure is glad you bought her
Because it's so lonely underwater!

Bought ___/___/___ for $_____.

'97
$35

45

M is for Maple...

MAPLE™

GBTru: $100 ↑1900%   **Item # 4600**

'97
$5

Issued: 1996 4 5
Status: Canadian Exclusive
Description: Bear with Maple Leaf flag. Canadian exclusive, commemorates Confederation Day. First pieces issued with name "Pride" on body tag. Maple with a Pride body tag has a GBTru of $350.00.
Birthday: 7/1/96
Poem: Maple the bear likes to ski
With his friends, he plays hockey.
He loves his pancakes and eats every crumb.
Can you guess which country he's from?
     Bought ___/___/___ for $_____.

MEL™

GBTru: $5 no change   **Item # 4162**

'97
$5

Issued: 1/1/97 4 5
Status: Current
Description: Grey koala bear.
Birthday: 1/15/96
Poem:
How do you name a Koala bear?
It's rather tough, I do declare!
It confuses me, I get in a funk
I'll name him Mel, after my favorite hunk!

     Bought ___/___/___ for $_____.

The best way to talk to Ty is through their website at www.ty.com.
The mailing address is:

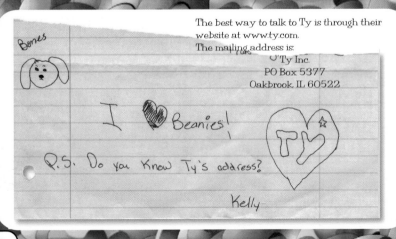

Bones

Ty Inc.
PO Box 5377
Oakbrook, IL 60522

I ♥ Beanies!

P.S. Do you Know Ty's address?

Kelly

Issued: 1994 ❤1 ❤2 ❤3

MYSTIC™ VERSION 1

Status: Out Of Production 1995

GBTru: $150 ↑50%   **Item #** 4007

Description: White unicorn with <u>tan horn</u>. Version 1: <u>Soft fine yarn</u> for mane and tail. Change to Version 2 in 1995.

Birthday: unknown

Poem: None.

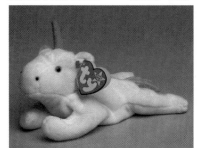

'97
$100

Bought ___/___/___ for $_____.

Issued: 1995 ❤3 ❤4

MYSTIC™ VERSION 2

Status: Out Of Production 1997

GBTru: $15 ↑200%   **Item #** 4007

Description: White unicorn with <u>tan horn</u>. Version 2: <u>Coarse yarn</u> for mane and tail. Change to Version 3 late 1997.

Birthday: 5/21/94

Poem:

Once upon a time in a land far away
A baby unicorn was born one day in May
Keep Mystic with you she's a prize
You'll see the magic in her blue eyes.

'97
$5

Bought ___/___/___ for $_____.

Issued: Late 1997 ❤4 ❤5

MYSTIC™ VERSION 3

Status: Current

GBTru: $5   **Item #** 4007

Description: White unicorn. Version 3: <u>Iridescent horn</u> with pink stitching.

Birthday: 5/21/94

Poem:

Once upon a time in a land far away
A baby unicorn was born one day in May
Keep Mystic with you she's a prize
You'll see the magic in her blue eyes.

Bought ___/___/___ for $_____.

N is for Nana...

NANA™

GBTru: $1200 ↑1100%   Item # 4067

'97
$100

Issued: 1995 ③
Status: Out Of Production 1995
Description: Monkey. The original Bongo. Nana has a #3 Swing Tag with a "Nana" sticker over the name "Bongo."
Birthday: unknown
Poem: None.

Bought ___/___/___ for $_____.

NANOOK™

GBTru: $5 no change   Item # 4104

'97
$5

Issued: 5/11/97 ④ ⑤
Status: Current
Description: Husky. Sled-dog.
Birthday: 11/21/96
Poem:
Nanook is a dog that loves cold weather
To him a sled is light as a feather
Over the snow and through the slush
He runs at hearing the cry of "mush!"

Bought ___/___/___ for $_____.

NIP™ VERSION 1

Issued: 1994

Status: Retired 1/1/98

Description: Gold cat. Version 1: Larger gold body with white triangle on face and <u>white belly</u>. Pink ears, nose and whiskers. Change to Version 2 in 1995.

Birthday: unknown

Poem: None.

GBTru: $350 ↑40%   Item # 4003

'97
$250

Bought ___/___/___ for $_____.

NIP™ VERSION 2

Issued: 1995

Status: Retired 1/1/98

Description: Gold cat. Version 2: Smaller <u>all gold body</u>. Pink ears and whiskers. Change to Version 3 in 1995.

Birthday: unknown

Poem: None.

GBTru: $675 ↑4%   Item # 4003

'97
$650

Bought ___/___/___ for $_____.

NIP™ VERSION 3

Issued: 1995

Status: Retired 1/1/98

Description: Gold cat. Version 3: Smaller gold body with <u>white paws</u>. Pink nose, white ears and whiskers.

Birthday: 3/6/94

Poem:

His name is Nipper, but we call him Nip
His best friend is a black cat named Zip
Nip likes to run in races for fun
He runs so fast he's always number one!

GBTru: $25 ↑400%   Item # 4003

'97
$5

Bought ___/___/___ for $_____.

N is for Nuts...

NUTS™

GBTru: $5 no change   Item # 4114

'97
$5

Issued: 1/1/97   **4**   **5**
Status: Current
Description: Brown squirrel.
Birthday: 1/21/96
Poem:
With his bushy tail, he'll scamper up a tree
The most cheerful critter you'll ever see.
He's nuts about nuts, and he loves to chat
Have you ever seen a squirrel like that?

Bought ___/___/___ for $_____.

PATTI™ VERSION 1

GBTru: $650 ↓57%   Item # 4025

'97
$1500

Issued: 1994   **1**   **2**   **3**
Status: Out Of Production 1995
Description: Platypus. One of the "Original 9." Version 1: Magenta. Also called Raspberry or Maroon. Change to Version 2 in 1995.
Birthday: unknown
Poem: None.

Bought ___/___/___ for $_____.

PATTI™ VERSION 2

GBTru: $5 no change   Item # 4025

'97
$5

Issued: 1995   **3**   **4**   **5**
Status: Current
Description: Platypus. One of the "Original 9." Version 2: Purple. This current version of Patti has the same fabric as Inch's tail. Also exists as a TBB.
Birthday: 1/6/93
Poem:
Ran into Patti one day while walking
Believe me she wouldn't stop talking!
Listened and listened to her speak
That would explain her extra large beak!

Bought ___/___/___ for $_____.

Issued: 5/11/97
Status: Current
Description: Tie-dye bear with peace symbol.
Birthday: 2/1/96
Poem:
All races, all colors, under the sun
Join hands together and have some fun
Dance to the music, rock and roll is the sound
Symbols of peace and love abound!

Bought ___/___/___ for $_____.

PEACE™

GBTru: $5 no change   Item # 4053

'97
$5

Issued: 1995
Status: Out Of Production 1995
Description: Elephant. Version 1: Royal blue with pale pink inner ears–issued and available for one shipment only in July 1995.
Birthday: unknown
Poem: None.

Bought ___/___/___ for $_____.

PEANUT™ VERSION 1

GBTru: $2,500 ↑25%   Item # 4062

'97
$2000

Issued: 1995
Status: Current
Description: Elephant. Version 2: Light blue.
Birthday: 1/25/95
Poem:
Peanut the elephant walks on tip-toes
Quietly sneaking wherever she goes
She'll sneak up on you and a hug you will get
Peanuts is a friend you won't soon forget.

Bought ___/___/___ for $_____.

PEANUT™ VERSION 2

GBTru: $5 no change   Item # 4062

'97
$5

P is for Peking...

PEKING™

GBTru: $900 ↑38%   **Item # 4013**

'97
$650

Issued: 1994 ❤ ❷ ❸
Status: Retired 1995
Description: Black and white panda bear.
Birthday: unknown
Poem: None.

Bought ___/___/___ for $_____.

PINCHERS™

GBTru: $5 no change   **Item # 4026**

'97
$5

Issued: 1994 ❤ ❷ ❸ ❹ ❺
Status: Current
Description: Red lobster. Successor to "Punchers." See page 55. One of the "Original 9."
Birthday: 6/19/93
Poem:
This lobster loves to pinch
Eating his food inch by inch
Balancing carefully with his tail
Moving forward slow as a snail!

Bought ___/___/___ for $_____.

PINKY™

GBTru: $5 no change   **Item # 4072**

'97
$5

Issued: 1995 ❸ ❹ ❺
Status: Current
Description: Pink flamingo. Also exists as a TBB.
Birthday: 2/13/95
Poem:
Pinky loves the Everglades
From the hottest pink she's made
With floppy legs and big orange beak
She's the Beanie that you seek!

Bought ___/___/___ for $_____.

POUCH™

Issued: 1/1/97

Status: Current

Description: Kangaroo with baby.

Birthday: 11/6/96

Poem:

My little pouch is handy I've found
It helps me carry my baby around
I hop up and down without any fear
Knowing my baby is safe and near.

GBTru: $5 no change   **Item # 4161**

'97
$5

Bought ___/___/___ for $_____.

POUNCE™

Issued: 1/1/98

Status: Current

Description: Chocolate brown cat with beige paws, inner ears and muzzle. Amber eyes, brown whiskers and pink nose.

Birthday: 8/28/97

Poem:

Sneaking and slinking down the hall
To pounce upon a fluffy yarn ball
Under the tables, around the chairs
Through the rooms and down the stairs!

GBTru: $5   **Item # 4122**

Bought ___/___/___ for $_____.

PRANCE™

Issued: 1/1/98

Status: Current

Description: Striped gray tabby w/white paws, inner ears & small traingle on face. Pink nose, whiskers and blue eyes.

Birthday: 11/20/97

Poem:

She darts around and swats the air
Then looks confused when nothing's there
Pick her up and pet her soft fur
Listen closely, and you'll hear her purr!

GBTru: $5   **Item # 4123**

Bought ___/___/___ for $_____.

P is for Princess...

PRINCESS™

GBTru: NE   Item # 4300

NE = Not Established

Issued: 10/29/97

Status: Current

Description: Royal purple bear, violet satin ribbon. White embroidered rose on chest. First Swing Tag reads, "All profits of Ty from this collectible will be donated to the DIANA, PRINCESS OF WALES MEMORIAL FUND."

Birthday: none

Poem:
Like an angel, she came from heaven above
She shared her compassion, her pain, her love
She only stayed with us long enough to teach
The world to share, to give, to reach.

Bought ___/___/___ for $_____.

PUFFER™

GBTru: $5   Item # 4181

Issued: 1/1/98

Status: Current

Description: Puffin has a black & white body & head w/red feet, orange & red beak.

Birthday: 11/3/97

Poem:
What in the world does a puffin do?
We're sure that you would like to know too
We asked Puffer how she spends her days
Before she answered, she flew away!

Bought ___/___/___ for $_____.

PUGSLY™

GBTru: $5 no change   Item # 4106

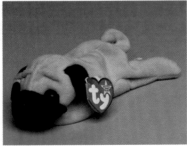

'97
$5

Issued: 5/11/97

Status: Current

Description: Cream pug dog with black ears and muzzle.

Birthday: 5/2/96

Poem:
Pugsly is picky about what he will wear
Never a spot, a stain or a tear
Image is something of which he'll gloat
Until he noticed his wrinkled coat!

Bought ___/___/___ for $_____.

PUNCHERS™

Issued: 1994 🎈

Status: Out Of Production 1994

Description: Red lobster. The original "Pinchers." See page 52. Aside from the name on the Swing Tag, the two lobsters are differentiated by the stitching on the tail. One of the "Original 9."

Birthday: unknown

Poem: None.

GBTru: $1200   Item # 4026

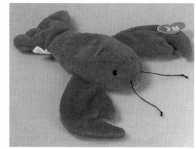

Bought ___/___/___ for $_____.

QUACKER™ VERSION 1

Issued: 1994 🎈 2️⃣

Status: Out Of Production 1994

Description: Yellow duck with orange bill and feet. Version 1: No wings.

Birthday: unknown

Poem: None.

GBTru: $1,400 ↓22%   Item # 4024

'97
$1800

Bought ___/___/___ for $_____.

QUACKERS™ VERSION 2

Issued: 1994 2️⃣ 3️⃣ 4️⃣ 5️⃣

Status: Current

Description: Yellow duck with orange bill and feet. Version 2: With wings. Also exists as TBB, "Quacks."

Birthday: 4/19/94

Poem:

There is a duck by the name of Quackers
Every night he eats animal crackers
He swims in a lake that's clear and blue
But he'll come to the shore to be with you!

GBTru: $5 no change   Item # 4024

'97
$5

Bought ___/___/___ for $_____.

R is for Radar...

RADAR™

GBTru: $100 ↑150%   Item # 4091

'97
$40

Issued: 1995 ③ ④
Status: Retired 5/11/97
Description: Black bat with red eyes.
Birthday: 10/30/95
Poem:
Radar the bat flies late at night
He can soar to an amazing height
If you see something as high as a star
Take a good look, it might be Radar!

Bought ___/___/___ for $_____.

RAINBOW™

GBTru: $5   Item # 4037

Issued: 1/1/98 ⑤
Status: Current
Description: Tie-dye chameleon
with blue head and collar to offset
yellow eyes and mouth.
Birthday: 10/14/97
Poem: Red, green, blue and yellow
This chameleon is a colorful fellow
A blend of colors, his own unique hue
Rainbow was made especially for
you!

Bought ___/___/___ for $_____.

REX™

GBTru: $350 ↑27%   Item # 4086

'97
$275

Issued: 1995 ③
Status: Retired 1996
Description: Tie-dye Tyrannosaurus
Rex.
Birthday: unknown
Poem: None.

Bought ___/___/___ for $_____.

RIGHTY™

Issued: 1996 🛡️

Status: Retired 1/1/97

Description: Grey elephant with American flag is symbol of the Republican Party.

Birthday: 7/4/96

Poem: Donkeys to the left, elephants to the right
Often seems like a crazy sight
This whole game seems very funny
Until you realize they're spending your money!

Bought ___/___/___ for $_____.

GBTru: $150 ↑200%   Item # 4086

'97
$50

RINGO™

Issued: 1995 🛡️3 🛡️4 🛡️5

Status: Current

Description: Brown raccoon.

Birthday: 7/14/95

Poem:
Ringo hides behind his mask
He will come out, if you should ask
He loves to chitter, he loves to chatter
Just about anything, it doesn't matter!

Bought ___/___/___ for $_____.

GBTru: $5 no change   Item # 4014

'97
$5

ROARY™

Issued: 5/11/97 🛡️4 🛡️5

Status: Current

Description: Lion. Hairy mane surrounds face. Tuft on tail.

Birthday: 2/20/96

Poem:
Deep in the jungle they crowned him king
But being brave is not his thing
A cowardly lion some may say
He hears his roar and runs away!

Bought ___/___/___ for $_____.

GBTru: $5 no change   Item # 4069

'97
$5

R is for Rover...

ROVER™

GBTru: $5 no change   Item # 4101

'97
$5

Issued: 1996
Status: Current
Description: Red dog.
Birthday: 5/30/96
Poem:
This dog is red and his name is Rover
If you call him he is sure to come over
He barks and plays with all his might
But worry not, he won't bite!

Bought ___/___/___ for $_____.

SCOOP™

GBTru: $5 no change   Item # 4107

'97
$5

Issued: 1996
Status: Current
Description: Grey pelican.
Birthday: 7/1/96
Poem:
All day long he scoops up fish
To fill his bill, is his wish
Diving fast and diving low
Hoping those fish are very slow!

Bought ___/___/___ for $_____.

SCOTTIE™

GBTru: $5 no change   Item # 4102

'97
$5

Issued: 1996
Status: Current
Description: Black terrier with curly-textured fabric.
Birthday: 6/15/96
Poem:
Scottie is a friendly sort
Even though his legs are short
He is always happy as can be
His best friends are you and me!

Bought ___/___/___ for $_____.

58

SEAMORE™

Issued: 1995

Status: Retired 10/1/97

GBTru: $75 ↑1400%   Item # 4029

Description: White seal. Also exists as a TBB.

Birthday: 12/14/96

Poem:

Seamore is a little white seal
Fish and clams are her favorite meal
Playing and laughing in the sand
She's the happiest seal in the land!

'97
$5

Bought ___/___/___ for $_____.

SEAWEED™

Issued: 1996 ③ ④ ⑤

Status: Current

GBTru: $5 no change   Item # 4080

Description: Otter holding clump of seaweed.

Birthday: 3/19/96

Poem:

Seaweed is what she likes to eat
It's supposed to be a delectable treat
Have you tried the treat from the water?
If you haven't maybe you "otter"!

'97
$5

Bought ___/___/___ for $_____.

SLITHER™

Issued: 1994 ① ② ③

Status: Retired 1995

GBTru: $950 ↑111%   Item # 4031

Description: Snake, almost 2 feet long, dark two-tone mottled top to resemble scales, yellow underside.

Birthday: unknown

Poem: None.

'97
$450

Bought ___/___/___ for $_____.

S is for Sly...

SLY™ VERSION 1

GBTru: $100 no change   Item # 4115

'97
$100

Issued: 1996 🛡
Status: Out Of Production 1996
Description: Fox. Version 1: <u>All brown</u> body. White inner ears and muzzle. Change to Version 2 in 1996.
Birthday: 9/12/96
Poem:
Sly is a fox and tricky is he
Please don't chase him, let him be
If you want him, just say when
He'll peek out from his den!

Bought ___/___/___ for $_____.

SLY™ VERSION 2

GBTru: $5 no change   Item # 4115

'97
$5

Issued: 1996 🛡 🛡
Status: Current
Description: Fox. Version 2: Brown body with <u>white belly</u>. White inner ears and muzzle.
Birthday: 9/12/96
Poem:
Sly is a fox and tricky is he
Please don't chase him, let him be
If you want him, just say when
He'll peek out from his den!

Bought ___/___/___ for $_____.

SMOOCHY™

GBTru: $5   Item # 4039

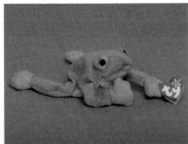

Issued: 1/1/98 🛡
Status: Current
Description: Green frog w/yellow "hands and feet" and prominent eyes.
Birthday: 10/1/97
Poem:
Is he a frog or maybe a prince?
This confusion makes him wince
Find the answer, help him with this
Be the one to give him a kiss!

Bought ___/___/___ for $_____.

SNIP™

Issued: 1/1/97 🛡️ 5️⃣

Status: Current

Description: Cream and brown Siamese cat.

Birthday: 10/22/96

Poem:
Snip the cat is Siamese
She'll be your friend if you please
So toss her a toy or a piece of string
Playing with you is her favorite thing.

Bought ___/___/___ for $_____.

GBTru: $5 no change   Item # 4120

'97
$5

SNORT™

Issued: 1/1/97 🛡️ 5️⃣

Status: Current

Description: Red bull with cream hooves, ears, and nose. Also exists as a TBB. Snort is the revised Tobasco. See Tobasco on page 69.

Birthday: 5/15/95

Poem:
Although Snort is not so tall
He loves to play basketball
He is a star player in his dreams
Can you guess his favorite team?

Bought ___/___/___ for $_____.

GBTru: $5 no change   Item # 4002

'97
$5

SNOWBALL™

Issued: 10/1/97 🛡️

Status: Retired 1/1/98

Description: Snowman w/orange nose, black hat & red scarf. Sewn on black mouth, shiny eyes & shiny black buttons.

Birthday: 12/22/96

Poem:
There is a snowman, I've been told
That plays with Beanies out in the cold
What is better out in a winter wonderland
Than a Beanie Snowman in your hand!

Bought ___/___/___ for $_____.

GBTru: $40   Item # 4201

S is for Sparky...

SPARKY™

GBTru: $55 ↑57%   **Item # 4100**

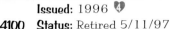

'97
$35

Issued: 1996
Status: Retired 5/11/97
Description: White and black Dalmatian.
Birthday: 2/27/96
Poem:
Sparky rides proud on the fire truck
Ringing the bell and pushing his luck
He gets underfoot when trying to help
He often gets stepped on and lets out a yelp!

Bought ___/___/___ for $_____.

SPEEDY™

GBTru: $25 ↑400%   **Item # 4030**

'97
$5

Issued: 1994
Status: Retired 10/1/97
Description: Green turtle. Also exists as a TBB.
Birthday: 8/14/94
Poem:
Speedy ran marathons in the past
Such a shame, always last
Now Speedy is a big star
After he bought a racing car.

Bought ___/___/___ for $_____.

SPIKE™

GBTru: $5 no change   **Item # 4060**

'97
$5

Issued: 1996
Status: Current
Description: Grey rhino.
Birthday: 8/13/96
Poem:
Spike the rhino loves to stampede
He's the bruiser that you need
Gentle to birds on his back and spike
You can be his friend if you like!

Bought ___/___/___ for $_____.

SPINNER™

Issued: 10/1/97

Status: Current

GBTru: $5   **Item # 4036**

Description: Spider with black head & legs. Gold & black striped body.

Birthday: 10/28/96

Poem:

Does this spider make you scared?
Among many people that feeling is shared
Remember spiders have feelings too
In fact, this spider really likes you!

Bought ___/___/___ for $_____.

SPLASH™

Issued: 1994

Status: Retired 5/11/97

GBTru: $65 ↑117%   **Item # 4022**

Description: Black and white orca whale. One of the "Original 9."

Birthday: 7/8/93

Poem:

Maybe it's because she sprained a limb
But Splash never learned how to swim
I'm sure Splash is happy that you caught her
Just be carefully not to leave her under water.

Alternate Poem:

Splash loves to jump and dive
He's the fastest whale alive
He always wins the 100 yard dash
With a victory jump he'll make a splash!

'97
$30

Splash joins Flash and Lizzy as a Beanie with two poems. Notice one is a *he* and one is a *she*!.

Dear Ms. Langenfeld:

   I just love "My First Greenbook" on Beanie Babies! It has so much information, I didn't realize there were so many versions, different colors, fabrics and styles of the older Beanies.

   I have a question on Splash. My Splash has a different poem than the one in the "Greenbook". Mine reads on the swing tag as follows:

        Splash loves to jump and dive
        He's the fastest whale alive
        He always wins the 100 yard dash
        With a victory jump he'll make a splash!

   Can you explain this variation?

                    Sincerely,

                    Teri

Bought ___/___/___ for $_____.

S is for Spook...

SPOOK™

GBTru: $150   Item # 4090

Issued: 1995 ❸
Status: Retired 1/1/98
Description: Ghost. The original "Spooky." Spook has a #3 Swing Tag with the name "Spook."
Birthday: unknown
Poem: None.

Bought ___ / ___ / ___ for $_____

SPOOKY™

GBTru: $40 ↑700%   Item # 4090

'97
$5

Issued: 1995 ❸ ❹
Status: Retired 1/1/98
Description: Ghost. Successor to "Spook." Exists with 3 different mouth styles. Black thread smile in V-shape, full-smile and half-smile.
Birthday: 10/31/95
Poem:
Ghosts can be a scary sight
But don't let Spooky bring you any fright
Because when you're alone, you will see
The best friend that Spooky can be!

Bought ___ / ___ / ___ for $_____

Emily
Lake Jackson, Tx-77566

Greenbook
P.O. Box 515
East Setauket, NY - 11733

"B.B Update"

Hannook
Snip
Peanut
Mel

Artwork by Emily Middleton

11733/0515 13

S is for Spot...

SPOT™ VERSION 1

Issued: 1994
Status: Retired 10/1/97
Description: White dog with black tail and ears. One of the "Original 9." Version 1: No spot on back. Change to Version 2 in 1994.
Birthday: unknown
Poem: None.

GBTru: $1400 ↓22%   Item # 4000

'97
$1800

Bought ___/___/___ for $_____.

SPOT™ VERSION 2

Issued: 1994
Status: Retired 10/1/97
Description: White dog with black tail and ears. One of the "Original 9." Version 2: Black spot on back.
Birthday: 1/3/93
Poem:
See Spot sprint, see Spot run
You and Spot can have lots of fun
Watch out now, because he's not slow
Just stand back and watch him go!

GBTru: $35 ↑600%   Item # 4000

'97
$5

Bought ___/___/___ for $_____.

SPUNKY™

Issued: 1/1/98
Status: Current
Description: Fawn colored cocker spaniel with feathery haired ears.
Birthday: 1/14/97
Poem:
Bouncing around without much grace
To jump on your lap and lick your face
But watch him closely, he has no fears
He'll run so fast, he'll trip over his ears!

GBTru: $5   Item # 4184

Bought ___/___/___ for $_____.

S is for Squealer...

SQUEALER™

GBTru: $5 no change   Item # 4005

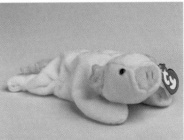

'97
$5

Issued: 1994 ❤1 ❤2 ❤3 ❤4 ❤5
Status: Current
Description: Pink pig. One of the "Original 9."
Birthday: 4/23/93
Poem:
Squealer likes to joke around
He is known as class clown
Listen to his stories for a while
There is no doubt he will make you smile!

Bought ___/___/___ for $_____.

STEG™

GBTru: $400 ↑78%   Item # 4087

'97
$225

Issued: 1995 ❤3
Status: Retired 1996
Description: Tie-dye Stegosaurus.
Birthday: unknown
Poem: None.

Bought ___/___/___ for $_____.

STING™

GBTru: $100 ↑100%   Item # 4077

'97
$50

Issued: 1995 ❤3 ❤4
Status: Retired 1/1/97
Description: Blue tie-dye manta ray.
Birthday: 8/27/95
Poem:
I'm a manta ray and my name is Sting
I'm quite unusual and this is the thing
Under the water I glide like a bird
Have you ever seen something so absurd?

Bought ___/___/___ for $_____.

STINKY™

Issued: 1995 ③ ④ ⑤
Status: Current
Description: Black and white skunk.
Birthday: 2/13/95
Poem:

Deep in the woods he lived in a cave
Perfume and mints were the gifts he gave
He showered every night in the kitchen sink
Hoping one day he wouldn't stink!

Bought ___/___/___ for $_____.

GBTru: $5 no change   Item # 4017

'97
$5

STRETCH™

Issued: 1/1/98 ⑤
Status: Current
Description: Ostrich w/ruff of feathery fabric at base of neck. Head & feet are beige. Body & wings are brown & ecru.
Birthday: 9/21/97
Poem: She thinks when her head is underground
The rest of her body can't be found
The Beanie Babies think it's absurd
To play hide and seek with this bird!

Bought ___/___/___ for $_____.

GBTru: $5   Item # 4182

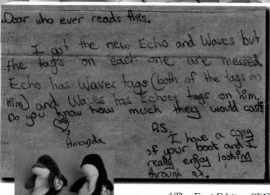

Dear who ever reads this,

I got the new Echo and Waves but the tags on each one are messed. Echo has Waves tags (both of the tags on him) and Waves has Echoes tags on him. Do you know how much they would cost?

♡, Amanda

P.S. I have a copy of your book and I really enjoy looking through at.

Echo the dolphin & Waves the whale were originally shipped mid-May '97 with each others' swing tag and body tag. This error confused many. What they were almost positive was a whale, had a poem that started out, "Echo the dolphin..." When the body tag matched the incorrect swing tag, many thought the likelihood was greater they didn't know dolphins from whales, than both tags were wrong! The First Edition GREENBOOK identified each correctly. Currently the mis-tagged Beanies are selling for $20.

67

S is for Stripes...

STRIPES™ VERSION 1

GBTru: $450 ↑13%   Item # 4065

'97
$400

Issued: 1995 🛡️
Status: Out Of Production 1995
Description: Gold and black tiger. Version 1: "Fuzzy Belly." Dark gold background and wide black stripes close together, different "fuzzier" fabric used on the underside. (Has B&W body tag.) Change to Version 2 in 1995.
Birthday: unknown
Poem: None.

Bought ___/___/___ for $_____.

STRIPES™ VERSION 2

GBTru: $200 ↓20%   Item # 4065

'97
$250

Issued: 1995 🛡️
Status: Out Of Production 1995
Description: Gold and black tiger. Version 2: Dark gold background with wide black stripes placed farther apart. (Has R&W body tag.) Change to Version 3 in 1995.
Birthday: unknown
Poem: None.

Bought ___/___/___ for $_____.

STRIPES™ VERSION 3

GBTru: $5 no change   Item # 4065

'97
$5

Issued: 1995 🛡️ 🛡️
Status: Current
Description: Gold and black tiger. Version 3: Light gold fabric with fewer narrow black stripes.
Birthday: 6/11/95
Poem:
Stripes was never fierce nor strong
So with tigers, he didn't get along
Jungle life was hard to get by
So he came to his friends at Ty.

Bought ___/___/___ for $_____.

STRUT™

Issued: 8/97 ♥ ♥

Status: Current

GBTru: $5   Item # 4171

Description: Rooster. Red crest, wings and tail on soft yellow tie-dye body. Replacement for "Doodle." See page 31.

Birthday: 3/8/96

Poem:

Listen closely to "Cock-a-doodle-doo"
What's the rooster saying to you?
Hurry, wake up sleepy head
We have lots to do, get out of bed!

Bought ___/___/___ for $_____.

TABASCO™

Issued: 1995 ♥ ♥

Status: Retired 1/1/97

GBTru: $195 ↓3%   Item # 4002

Description: Red bull with white nose. Reintroduced as Snort with small changes. See Snort on page 61.

Birthday: 5/15/95

Poem:

Although Tabasco is not so tall
He loves to play basketball
He is a star player in his dream
Can you guess his favorite team?

'97
$200

Bought ___/___/___ for $_____.

Mid 1997 the body tags were changed to include a star in the upper left corner. Apparently, during the transition between no-star and star body tags, a clear sticker

Dear _____,

Hi my name is Andrea I live in Gig Harbor Washingtion

Im ceriose about Strips3 because he has a star by ty sign on the back tag. Me and my cousien share becau s e have more this way. Im also ceouris about Mel becau s e your first green book and it says that that Mel isent retired but I heard that he is. So if the star means anythin or Mel is retired pleas! teel me.

with only the star printed on it was placed on no-star body tags over the Ty heart so that the star appears in the upper left corner (See page 13.)

T is for Tank...

TANK™ VERSION 1

GBTru: $150 ↑50%   Item # 4031

'97
$100

Issued: 1995 🛡️
Status: Retired 10/1/97
Description: Grey armadillo. Version 1: Greater bean fill and 7 plated shell lines. No shell. Change to Version 2 mid-1996.
Birthday: unknown
Poem: None.

Bought ___/___/___ for $_____.

TANK™ VERSION 2

GBTru: $295 ↑97%   Item # 4031

'97
$150

Issued: 1996 🛡️ 🛡️
Status: Retired 10/1/97
Description: Grey armadillo. Version 2: Less bean fill and 9 plated shell lines. Still no shell. Change to Version 3 in 1996.
Birthday: 2/22/95
Poem:
This armadillo lives in the South
Shoving Tex-Mex in his mouth
He sure loves it south of the border
Keeping his friends in good order!

Bought ___/___/___ for $_____.

TANK™ VERSION 3

GBTru: $50 ↑900%   Item # 4031

'97
$5

Issued: 1996 🛡️
Status: Retired 10/1/97
Description: Grey armadillo. Version 3: Smaller body with 7 or 9 plated shell lines and shell.
Birthday: 2/22/95
Poem:
This armadillo lives in the South
Shoving Tex-Mex in his mouth
He sure loves it south of the border
Keeping his friends in good order!

Bought ___/___/___ for $_____.

Issued: 1994 ❤ ❷
Status: Retired 10/1/97
Description: Brown bear. Old pointed face, eyes set wide apart and small nose. Change to New Face in 1994.
Birthday: unknown
Poem: None.

TEDDY™ BROWN
OLD FACE

GBTru: $1200 ↑200%   **Item # 4050**

'97
$400

Bought ___ / ___ / ___ for $_____.

Issued: 1994 ❷ ❸ ❹
Status: Retired 10/1/97
Description: Brown bear. New round face, with eyes set closer together, burgundy neck ribbon.
Birthday: 11/28/95
Poem:
Teddy wanted to go out today
All his friends went out to play
But he'd rather help whatever you do
After all, his best friend is you!

TEDDY™ BROWN
NEW FACE

GBTru: $50 ↑900%   **Item # 4050**

'97
$5

Bought ___ / ___ / ___ for $_____.

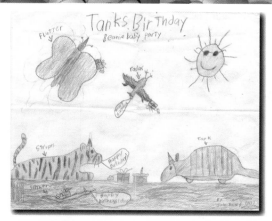

by John

T is for Teddy...

TEDDY™ CRANBERRY OLD FACE

GBTru: $900 ↑200%   Item # 4052

'97
$300

Issued: 1994 ❤ ❷
Status: Retired 1995
Description: Cranberry bear. Old pointed face, eyes set wide apart and small nose. Change to New Face in 1994.
Birthday: unknown
Poem: None.

Bought ___/___/___ for $_____

TEDDY™ CRANBERRY NEW FACE

GBTru: $950 ↑138%   Item # 4052

'97
$400

Issued: 1994 ❷ ❸
Status: Retired 1995
Description: Cranberry bear. New round face, with eyes set closer together, green neck ribbon.
Birthday: unknown
Poem: None.

Bought ___/___/___ for $_____

TEDDY™ JADE OLD FACE

GBTru: $850 ↑209%   Item # 4057

'97
$275

Issued: 1994 ❤ ❷
Status: Retired 1995
Description: Dark green bear. Old pointed face, eyes set wide apart and small nose. Change to New Face in 1994.
Birthday: unknown
Poem: None.

Bought ___/___/___ for $_____

TEDDY™ JADE
NEW FACE

Issued: 1994 2️ 3️
Status: Retired 1995
Description: Dark green bear. New round face, with eyes set closer together, maroon neck ribbon.
Birthday: unknown
Poem: None.

GBTru: $900 ↑177%   Item # 4057

'97
$325

Bought ___/___/___ for $_____.

TEDDY™ MAGENTA
OLD FACE

Issued: 1994 ❤️ 2️
Status: Retired 1995
Description: Magenta bear. Old pointed face, eyes set wide apart and small nose. Change to New Face in 1994.
Birthday: unknown
Poem: None.

GBTru: $900 ↑125%   Item # 4056

'97
$400

Bought ___/___/___ for $_____.

TEDDY™ MAGENTA
NEW FACE

Issued: 1994 2️ 3️
Status: Retired 1995
Description: Magenta bear. New round face, with eyes set closer together, pink neck ribbon.
Birthday: unknown
Poem: None.

GBTru: $950 ↑58%   Item # 4056

'97
$600

Bought ___/___/___ for $_____.

73

TEDDY™ TEAL
OLD FACE

GBTru: $900 ↑125%   Item # 4051

'97
$400

Issued: 1994
Status: Retired 1995
Description: Green bear. Old pointed face, eyes set wide apart and small nose. Change to New Face in 1994.
Birthday: unknown
Poem: None.

Bought ___/___/___ for $_____

TEDDY™ TEAL
NEW FACE

GBTru: $1100 ↑83%   Item # 4051

'97
$600

Issued: 1994
Status: Retired 1995
Description: Green bear. New round face, with eyes closer together, blue neck ribbon.
Birthday: unknown
Poem: None.

Bought ___/___/___ for $_____

TEDDY™ VIOLET
OLD FACE

GBTru: $1000 ↑150%   Item # 4055

'97
$400

Issued: 1994
Status: Retired 1995
Description: Violet bear. Old pointed face, eyes set wide apart and small nose. Change to New Face in 1994.
Birthday: unknown
Poem: None.

Bought ___/___/___ for $_____

Issued: 1994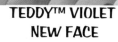
Status: Retired 1995
Description: Violet bear. New round face, with eyes closer together, green neck ribbon.
Birthday: unknown
Poem: None.

TEDDY™ VIOLET
NEW FACE

GBTru: $1100 ↑69%   Item # 4055

'97
$650

Bought ___/___/___ for $_____.

Issued: 1994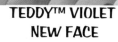
Status: Retired 1995
Description: Grey mouse with pink tail, feet, nose and inner ears. Eyes and whiskers are black.
Birthday: unknown
Poem: None.

TRAP™

GBTru: $700 ↑100%   Item # 4042

'97
$350

Bought ___/___/___ for $_____.

Issued: 5/11/97
Status: Current
Description: Terrier. Dark and light brown pup. Curly-textured fabric.
Birthday: 10/12/96
Poem:
Taking off with a thunderous blast
Tuffy rides his motorcycle fast
The Beanies roll with laughs & squeals
He never took off his training wheels!

TUFFY™

GBTru: $5 no change   Item # 4108

'97
$5

Bought ___/___/___ for $_____.

TUSK™

GBTru: $50 no change   Item # 4076

'97
$50

Issued: 1995 ❸ ❹
Status: Retired 1/1/97
Description: Walrus. Small quantity found with misprint 'Tuck' body tag. Some early pieces had up-turned tusks.
Birthday: 9/18/95
Poem: Tusk brushes his teeth everyday
To keep them shiny, it's the only way
Teeth are special, so you must try
And they will sparkle when you say "Hi"!

Bought ___/___/___ for $_____.

TWIGS™

GBTru: $5 no change   Item # 4068

'97
$5

Issued: 1995 ❸ ❹ ❺
Status: Current
Description: Orange and gold giraffe.
Birthday: 5/19/95
Poem:
Twigs has his head in the clouds
He stands tall, he stands proud
With legs so skinny they wobble and shake
What an unusual friend he will make!

Bought ___/___/___ for $_____.

VALENTINO™

GBTru: $5 no change   Item # 4058

'97
$5

Issued: 1994 ❷ ❸ ❹ ❺
Status: Current
Description: White bear has red embroidered heart on chest. Note Valentine Birthday.
Birthday: 2/14/94
Poem:
His heart is red and full of love
He cares for you so give him a hug
Keep him close when feeling blue
Feel the love he has for you!

Bought ___/___/___ for $_____.

VELVET™

Issued: 1995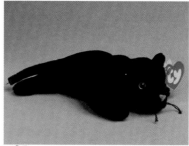

Status: Retired 10/1/97

GBTru: $20 ↑300%   Item # 4064

Description: Black panther.

Birthday: 12/16/95

Poem:

Velvet loves to sleep in the trees
Lulled to dreams by the bees
She snoozes all day and plays all night
Running and jumping in the moonlight!

'97
$5

Bought ___/___/___ for $_____.

WADDLE™

Issued: 1995

GBTru: $5 no change   Item # 4075

Status: Current

Description: Black and white penguin.

Birthday: 12/19/95

Poem:

Waddle the penguin likes to dress up
Every night he wears his tux
When Waddle walks, it never fails
He always trips over his tails!

'97
$5

Bought ___/___/___ for $_____.

WAVES™

Issued: 5/11/97

GBTru: $5 no change   Item # 4084

Status: Current

Description: Whale. Black with white underbelly. Echo and Waves were originally shipped with each others swing tag and body tag. See page 67.

Birthday: 12/8/96

Poem:

Join him today on the Internet
Don't be afraid to get your feet wet
He taught all the Beanies how to surf
Our web page is his home turf!

'97
$5

Bought ___/___/___ for $_____.

WEB™

↑114%   Item # 4041

'97
$350

Issued: 1994 🛡 🛡 🛡
Status: Retired 1995
Description: Black spider with red belly.
Birthday: unknown
Poem: None.

Bought ___/___/___ for $_____.

WEENIE™

GBTru: $5 no change   Item # 4013

'97
$5

Issued: 1996 🛡 🛡 🛡
Status: Current
Description: Brown Dachshund.
Birthday: 7/20/95
Poem:
Weenie the dog is quite a sight
Long of body and short of height
He perches himself high on a log
And considers himself to be top dog!

Bought ___/___/___ for $_____.

WRINKLES™

GBTru: $5 no change   Item # 4103

'97
$5

Issued: 1996 🛡 🛡
Status: Current
Description: Tan and white Old English Bull dog.
Birthday: 5/1/96
Poem:
This little dog is named Wrinkles
His nose is soft and often crinkles
Likes to climb up on your lap
He's a cheery sort of chap!

Bought ___/___/___ for $_____.

Issued: 1995 ③ ④ ⑤

Status: Current

Description: Black and white zebra.

Birthday: 12/24/95

Poem:

Ziggy likes soccer—he's a referee
That way he watches the games for free
The other Beanies don't think it's fair
But Ziggy the zebra doesn't care.

Bought ___/___/___ for $_____

ZIGGY™

GBTru: $5 no change   **Item # 4063**

'97
$5

OTHER GUIDES FROM GREENBOOK

GREENBOOK Guide to
The Enesco Precious Moments Collection

GREENBOOK Guide to
Department 56 Villages including
The Original Snow Village and
The Heritage Village Collections

GREENBOOK Guide to
Department 56 Snowbabies

GREENBOOK Guide to
Hallmark Keepsake Ornaments

GREENBOOK Guide to
Hallmark Kiddie Car Classics

GREENBOOK Guide to
The Walt Disney Classics Collection

GREENBOOK Guide to
Cherished Teddies by Enesco

GREENBOOK Guide to
Precious Moments Company Dolls

GREENBOOK Guide to
Harbour Lights

GREENBOOK Guide to
Boyds Bears

GREENBOOK Guide to
Charming Tails

for Zip...

™ VERSION 1

↑17%   Item # 4004

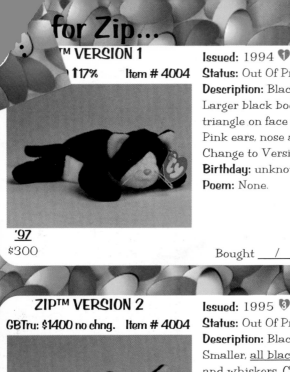

'97
$300

Issued: 1994
Status: Out Of Production 1995
Description: Black cat. Version 1:
Larger black body with white
triangle on face and <u>white belly</u>.
Pink ears, nose and whiskers.
Change to Version 2 in 1995.
Birthday: unknown
Poem: None.

Bought ___/___/___ for $_____.

ZIP™ VERSION 2

GBTru: $1400 no chng.   Item # 4004

'97
$1400

Issued: 1995
Status: Out Of Production 1995
Description: Black cat. Version 2:
Smaller, <u>all black body</u>. Pink ears
and whiskers. Change to Version 3
in 1995.
Birthday: unknown
Poem: None.

Bought ___/___/___ for $_____.

ZIP™ VERSION 3

GBTru: $5 no change   Item # 4004

'97
$5

Issued: 1995
Status: Current
Description: Black cat. Version 3:
Smaller black body with <u>white paws</u>.
White ears and whiskers, pink nose.
Birthday: 3/28/94
Poem: Keep Zip by your side all the
day through
Zip is good luck, you'll see it's true
When you have something you
need to do
Zip will always believe in you!

Bought ___/___/___ for $_____.

In April of 1997, McDonald's began what was to be a 5-week Happy Meal promotion with two different Teenie Beanie designs being offered each week.

Despite production of 100 million Teenie Beanies, demand far exceeded supply and, in many places around the country, restaurants sold out of the entire five week supply in just 3 days!

Teenie Beanies are also referred to as "McBeanies" and "TBB's."

Teenie Beanies are about 1/3 the size of regular Beanies and have a single heart swing tag. Because the toy was for children of all ages, for safety, they have embroidered eyes, nose...

The item # appears on the plastic bag they are packaged in, but not on the swing tag or body tag.

Teenie Beanies have no Suggested Retail Price. They were free with the purchase of a Happy Meal.

Issued: 4/97
Status: Happy Meal Promotion
Description: Brown moose with orange antlers.
Birthday: unknown
Poem: None.

CHOCOLATE™

GBTru: $12 ↑20%   Item # 4

'97
$10

Bought ___/___/___ for $_____.

CHOPS™

GBTru: $15 ↑25%   Item # 3

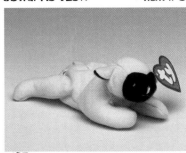

'97
$12

Issued: 4/97
Status: Happy Meal Promotion
Description: Cream lamb with black face and inner ears.
Birthday: unknown
Poem: None.

Bought ___/___/___ for $_____.

GOLDIE™

GBTru: $8 no change   Item # 5

'97
$8

Issued: 4/97
Status: Happy Meal Promotion
Description: Goldfish.
Birthday: unknown
Poem: None.

Bought ___/___/___ for $_____.

LIZZ™

GBTru: $12 no change   Item # 10

'97
$12

Issued: 4/97
Status: Happy Meal Promotion
Description: Lizard.
Birthday: unknown
Poem: None.

Bought ___/___/___ for $_____.

PATTI™

Issued: 4/97
Status: Happy Meal Promotion
Description: Purple platypus.
Birthday: unknown
Poem: None.

GBTru: $20 ↑43%   Item # 1

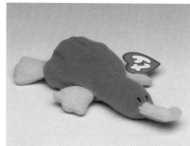

'97
$14

Bought ___/___/___ for $_____.

PINKY™

Issued: 4/97
Status: Happy Meal Promotion
Description: Pink flamingo.
Birthday: unknown
Poem: None.

GBTru: $25 ↑56%   Item # 2

'97
$16

Bought ___/___/___ for $_____.

QUACKS™

Issued: 4/97
Status: Happy Meal Promotion
Description: Yellow duck.
Birthday: unknown
Poem: None.

GBTru: $8 no change   Item # 9

'97
$8

Bought ___/___/___ for $_____.

Teenie Beanies

SEAMORE™

GBTru: $10 ↑25% **Item # 7**

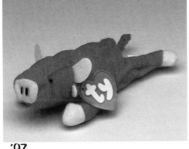

'97
$8

Issued: 4/97
Status: Happy Meal Promotion
Description: White seal.
Birthday: unknown
Poem: None.

Bought ___/___/___ for $_____.

SNORT™

GBTru: $12 no change **Item # 8**

'97
$12

Issued: 4/97
Status: Happy Meal Promotion
Description: Red bull.
Birthday: unknown
Poem: None.

Bought ___/___/___ for $_____.

SPEEDY™

GBTru: $8 no change **Item # 6**

'97
$8

Issued: 4/97
Status: Happy Meal Promotion
Description: Green turtle.
Birthday: unknown
Poem: None.

Bought ___/___/___ for $_____.

Exclusive Beanies

In more and more instances,
Beanie Babies are being used as promotional items
for sporting events, fundraisers, etc.
Organizations are buying cases of a particular Beanie
and adding their own little touches.
GREENBOOK limits listings in the Guide
to promotions
sanctioned by Ty.

CHICAGO CUBS CUBBIE™ PROMOTION 5/18/97

GBTru: $150*

Description: First 10,000 children under the age of 13 attending the Cubs vs. Giants on 5/18/97 were given Cubbie with a commemorative card. Sponsored by Pepsi. *GBTru for Cubbie w/Commemorative Card. Without the card, it's just a Cubbie.

Birthday: 11/14/93

Poem: Cubbie used to eat crackers and honey
And what happened to him was funny
He was stung by fourteen bees
Now Cubbie eats broccoli and cheese!

Bought ___/___/___ for $_____.

CHICAGO CUBS CUBBIE™ PROMOTION 9/6/97

GBTru: $125*

Description: First 10,000 children under the age of 13 attending the Cubs vs. Mets on 9/6/97 were given Cubbie with a commemorative card. Sponsored by Pepsi. *GBTru for Cubbie w/Commemorative Card. Without the card, it's just a Cubbie.

Birthday: 11/14/93

Poem: Cubbie used to eat crackers and honey
And what happened to him was funny
He was stung by fourteen bees
Now Cubbie eats broccoli and cheese!

Bought ___/___/___ for $_____.

Exclusive Beanies

EMPLOYEE CHRISTMAS BEARS

GBTru: $2,500/each

Description: Employee gift at Christmas party. New Face Violet Bear with either green or red satin ribbon. No Swing Tag. R&W body tag with no name.
Birthday: unknown
Poem: None.

Bought ___/___/___ for $_____

SPECIAL OLYMPICS MAPLE™

GBTru: $300

Issued: August 1997 🛡4

Description: Fund raiser for the Canadian Special Olympics. Maple #4600 – In addition to the heart Ty Swing Tag there's a round tag that reads "Special Olympics Sports Celebrities Festival" and includes the Special Olympics oath, "Let me win, but if I cannot win, let me be brave in the attempt."
Birthday: 7/1/96
Poem: Maple the bear likes to ski
With his friends, he plays hockey.
He loves his pancakes and eats every crumb.
Can you guess which country he's from?

Bought ___/___/___ for $_____

Item# Index

ITEM # INDEX

Picture Gallery Index

88

Picture Gallery Index

89

Picture Gallery Index

Picture Gallery Index

Picture Gallery Index

Picture Gallery Index

Picture Gallery Index

Picture Gallery Index

Picture Gallery Index

ERIN™

As we were going to press, Ty announced a new Beanie Baby. Here is the information we have on this St. Patrick's Day bear.

Birthday: 3/17/97

Poem:
Named after the beautiful Emerald Isle
This Beanie Baby will make you smile,
A bit of luck, a pot of gold,
Light up the faces, both young and old!

Bought _____ / _____ / _____ for $_____